M000031042

Nothing Happens Till Somebody Sells Something

DAVID A. STONE

BRISA BOOKS

ISBN-10:0987727427
ISBN-13: 97809877274-2-8
Published by Brisa Books, an imprint of
WindWord Communications Inc.
#509, 4438 West 10th Avenue
Vancouver, British Columbia, Canada
www.brisabooks.com

For Gail, who dares to dream with me

FOREWORD

The other day a friend told me that I am 'deliberately disruptive.' I took it as a compliment.

This book intends to be as disruptive, unsettling and thought provoking as possible. Why? Because the design professions are like that frog in the pot of water where someone keeps turning up the heat. We're quietly going to boil to death if someone doesn't jump soon.

The AE industry is about as mature and set in its ways as it gets. Let's face it, the Assyrians were building roads, bridges, water systems, and elaborate buildings too. We're just carrying on with a very long tradition. Our tools are more sophisticated (and expensive!) but our methods of doing business haven't evolved very far.

Back in the mid-70's when I first started in this business, it was considered unethical to publish even a business card as an advertisement. You could get called in and your knuckles rapped for such unprofessional conduct! Today we're in a knock-'em down, drag-it-out fight over pennies as clients drive the industry further and further into commodity status. Somebody has to pull the rug out from underneath us if we're to survive and thrive into the future.

I remember back in architecture school when they told us that if we just did our work well enough, everything would take care of itself. It was a barefaced lie. It's my intention in this book to call out that lie, rattle our comfortable cages and sweet-talk, scare, bribe, cajole and otherwise persuade you in any way I can to think about a different way of marketing and selling your design services.

Cuz I'm really not that into boiled frog.

David Stone, June, 2014

Contents

Improving your marketing ROI	12
Getting the highest return in the planning phase	14
Investing in brand-building	16
Maximizing your ROI on the Go/No Go decision	18
ROI on boldness	20
Do you stand out in the crowd?	22
Client focus and customer service	25
Does social media belong in your marketing plan?	26
The secret to a great client debrief	28
Closed Jobs Analysis	30
Keep a "dossier" on your competitors	32
Timeless wisdom	34
So you're in it for the money	36
Why your attempts to use CRM aren't working	40
When does your Loss-Free Day occur?	42
The story of the $1 million fee	44
Avoiding the Trite Trap	46
So what?	48
Keeping clients for life	50
The project that wasn't there	54
Making a great first impression	56
Are you running a country club?	63
Let's talk about commodities	65
Hourly rates	68
Is anyone paying attention?	71

Keeping your audience's attention 73

Raising the Attention-O-Meter 75

Why aren't you paid more? 76

And that means… 78

Left brain, right brain – Let's go marketing 80

Light a fire in your presentation 82

Why it's so easy to sell Volvos 84

Your brand is NOT… 86

Practical market research 89

The five obligations of a marketing department 91

The important thing to leave behind after a presentation 94

Lessons from Walt Disney 96

Do logos, colors and company names matter? 98

We can all improve our game 100

Thinking outside the awards box 102

A fitness test for your mailing list 104

Direct mail — it ain't always junk 107

The storekeeper 109

Personal business development plans 111

Business development is like love 113

One more thing… 115

Acknowledgments

As FDR once said, "Above all, try something."

This book is dedicated to the hundreds of design and construction firms — big, small and in-between — from whom I've learned untold lessons about what works, what stopped working long ago, and the magic that can be accomplished when you cross your fingers and just try something.

Improving your marketing ROI:
How to get the most for the least and measure your results

Many CEO's and CFO's are asking hard questions of their marketing teams regarding the spending of scarce dollars in the effort to win new work. And so they should! As much as the marketers might squirm under the spotlight, the questions are legitimate and need to be asked. If spending can't be justified with a clear return it should be cut off.

That said, marketing ROI is traditionally hard to measure since it's very difficult to assign clear results to any particular undertaking. That new client may have first heard of your firm from an award you won, then learned more about you through your direct mail program, been impressed as one of your team members spoke at a conference, then made the final decision when your well-written proposal was competitively priced. While each of these initiatives contributed to the win, it's impossible to allocate the exact amounts that resulted in the win.

Nonetheless there are very clear guidelines that will help you get the most from your marketing dollars and there are useful ways to measure your return.

Instead of thinking about marketing as one non-stop endeavor, the 'win work' effort should be viewed as a series of four consecutive steps that ultimately lead to a new client and a fifth step that will ensure they stick around in a long-term relationship:

Five steps to winning work
1. Strategic and marketing planning
2. Brand-building
3. Business development
4. Responding to RFPs
5. Customer Service

While your ultimate goal is a client with signed contracts, no single one of these steps will produce that result. So your return on a brand-building effort, for example, shouldn't be measured by the number of new projects you sign in a year. Each step has its own clear goals and your measurements should focus on how well you achieved that goal.

In the sections that follow we'll look at each of these areas in turn and identify how you can maximize the return on your marketing investment.

Getting the highest return in the planning phase

Your clients understand that it's worthwhile to invest in your services to plan their projects. So you should understand the tremendous value in creating and following an intelligent plan for your marketing efforts. Far too many firms still use an approach that can best be described as, 'if it moves, we'll shoot at it.'

While no plan ever remains static from its first iteration, the planning process forces you to think about how you will allocate the finite resources you have available for marketing and ensure the effort isn't wasted.

The highest-value strategy you can take in the planning process is one that narrows and focuses your marketing efforts instead of spreading and diversifying them. While this may seem counter-intuitive — and it's certainly opposite to what many firms do — there is no question that focus produces a higher ROI than diversification.

Imagine you are a military General on a battlefield with 5,000 troops at your disposal. Is it better to spread them out in a long line and charge every enemy position, or to concentrate your forces on one or two targets at a time? Obviously, if you dilute your resources too greatly, the impact you'll have on your target markets becomes negligible, producing a very low ROI.

The best strategy is to analyze your target markets, determine the 'sweet spots' (those areas where you are most likely to have success), and focus the bulk of your efforts on those. Does this mean that you'll ignore opportunities from other market sectors? No. But you can treat those in an opportunistic manner, rather than as a key target market.

There is an old marketing rule of thumb I like to call the 'Rule of Five.' It suggests that at any time you have five target markets. Of these, three are strong and vital and responsible for the bulk of your revenues. One is a new and emerging market that you're beginning to invest in and expect to be a solid producer in two or three years. And the final one is an older, mature market that no longer provides the same returns as it once did. Two or three years from now you likely won't be serving that marketing any more.

When you build your marketing plan, avoid broad generalizations. Instead, make it specific with 'what-we'll-do-on-Monday-morning' activities:

We will be targeting municipalities with populations between 20,000 and 200,000 in the three surrounding states, aiming to win water and wastewater projects. To accomplish this we will be using a combination of direct mail and email, attendance at targeted conferences at which we will deliver cutting-edge technical papers, and we will launch an aggressive relationship-building effort with the Public Works Directors in this list of 25 municipalities.

Measuring ROI on the planning effort is tricky. But the best and most fundamental thing you can do is to answer two simple questions:

1. Do we have a detailed marketing plan for the next 12-24 months?
2. Are we executing the elements of that plan in accordance with the schedule we established?

If you answer 'no' to either or both of those questions, you are getting a very poor return on your planning effort. You invested the effort and now you're doing nothing about it. ROI doesn't get lower than that.

If you answer 'yes' to both those questions, you WILL be achieving a high return on your planning investment. You WILL be making a positive impression in those markets and you WILL see results.

Investing in brand-building

First, let's define what we're talking about when we say 'brand-building.' This is the effort you expend to establish a wide-spread knowledge and understanding of the facts that your firm exists and what it does (name-recognition), that your firm is well-regarded within your target markets (reputation-enhancement) and that the decision makers and influencers within your target markets are familiar with and have a positive view of your firm, whether they've ever actually worked with you or not (marketers call this, "mind share.")

Traditionally, a design firm's brand has been established over a long period of time, mostly by word of mouth, and is almost exclusively restricted to the clients with which you've worked. Very often, outside that circle of clients, the firm's name is hardly known at all. But a strong brand name is essential for a firm to thrive today and it's no longer enough to rely on the slow pace of word-of-mouth advertising. A firm must take a proactive approach to establish its brand throughout its target market.

A well-designed and executed brand-building program 'surrounds' every decision-maker and influencer in your target market with reminders of your firm. When they go through their mail, you're there. When they attend their conferences, you're there. When they read their industry journals, you're there. When they open their in-box, you're there. After 12 months or more of this, especially when the high-quality content of your communication shows you to be an industry thought leader, they'll have easily reached the conclusion that they owe it to themselves to include you in their list of preferred providers.

The best return on your branding investment comes through regular, frequent and broadly-cast communications to your entire market. This includes those who have never been clients — even the clients of your competitors! The worst use of your resources is to send information irregularly and infrequently. The firm that sends an annual holiday card, or three issues of a newsletter followed by silence, would be better off doing nothing and saving the time and cost.

Since the goal of brand-building is to raise the knowledge and understanding of your firm throughout your market, the best way to measure the effectiveness of the effort is to conduct regular surveys of the market to see how much that knowledge has been raised. A simple perception survey, conducted annually, will provide clear data on the results of your campaign. If perception and understanding are going up, your efforts are working.

Measuring ROI is also a simple matter. Most firms obtain between 70% and 90% of their revenue from repeat clients. Presumably, those clients don't come back because of your brand-building efforts. They already know the firm. By tracking new client activity, and making a point to determine how the new clients first heard about the firm, you can gauge the return on your branding investment. If you spend $25,000 in a year for brand-building and it attracts one new client with a $50,000 project, your ROI is 200% in the first year. If that client sticks around with additional projects, your ROI goes higher still.

Maximizing your ROI on the Go/No Go decision

How would you like to double your hit rate — and therefore your ROI — overnight? Simple: just cut in half the number of RFPs you respond to and proposals you submit.

Jokes aside, virtually every firm I've dealt with writes too many proposals. In a world where relationships are key, far too many firms get suckered into submitting expensive proposals they have no chance of winning. Your first step in writing a proposal that is wired to win is to stop writing ones that are likely to lose.

But the decision of whether or not to chase a project is a tough one. It's a guarantee that if you don't chase it, you won't win it. As a result, many firms shoot at anything that moves, figuring that if they submit enough proposals they're bound to win something.

They treat it as a simple numbers game. Unfortunately it's also an expensive, time-consuming and frustrating process that usually produces those good news/bad news results: the good news is you won a project. The bad news is that it's with *that* unreasonable client, under those ridiculous contract terms, to design that questionable project.

Among the many advantages of cutting down the number of proposals you write is the fact that you'll now have the time to invest in proper research, writing, designing and producing a much higher quality proposal. No more of those last minute panics as you wonder if the search-and-replace function in MS Word has actually found all instances of the name of the last client to whom you sent this same proposal last week.

Imagine how much better your proposal will look and read when it's the only one due this Friday instead of the three that you've often had to juggle before. And there are even more benefits to cutting down the number of proposals you write:

- You get to choose the clients who are a good fit for your firm.
- The stress levels for you and your marketing team go way down.

- Fewer mistakes are made in the proposal documents and you'll have time for the quality control that can catch those few goof-ups.
- Your proposals will be precisely targeted to each specific opportunity rather than a generic re-write of something similar.
- By turning down poorly aligned opportunities, you position your firm more strongly in the marketplace.
- Your overhead costs for proposal writing will be lower.
- You'll have more time to spend building and reinforcing relationships that turn into sole-source or preferred provider work and reduce or eliminate competition.

It's always tempting to go after that questionable job: What if there are no more jobs out there? What if our backlog shrinks further? How will I keep all these employees busy? While these fears are real, our imaginations tend to make them much more frightening than they actually are. In fact, increasing the quality and focus of the proposals you choose to write is a much more effective way of dealing with these risks anyway.

The ROI calculation is simple:

Total revenue from projects on which your proposal won ÷ proposal costs

Now recalculate using a denominator that is half that size. That's a better number, isn't it!

ROI on boldness

Now let's focus on making the proposals that you DO write knock the socks off those people who are about to become your new clients. If you want to make the short list you have two strategy choices:

1. Play it safe and avoid offending anyone who might give your firm a black mark. This is the defensive strategy.

2. Grab their attention by the throat, throw them to the ground with your laser-focused response and take an aggressive approach that leaves them absolutely no choice but to include you on the short list. This is the offensive tactic.

Since every good coach knows the best defense is a good offense, we're going to use the second strategy to win this particular game.

Your aggressive game plan will use a three-pronged strategy:

1. It must be bold.
2. It must differentiate you from your competition.
3. It must be client-centered.

Let's start by looking at the boldness of your proposals.

There is nothing easier in the A/E industry than to come second in a project selection process. It must be easy because so many firms regularly accomplish it!

You never hear, "we came fifth!" All the time it's, "we came second." Or how about, "We came a close second!" (as if that paid more than 'regular' second.) The point is, in this business, you either win or you lose. There is no such thing as second place, just one winner, and a whole string of losers.

I believe very strongly that the riskiest thing a firm can do today is to be normal, predictable and 'safe.' Why is that risky? Because you'll end up looking exactly like every other firm with which you are competing. And that road leads to commodity pricing.

Right now, stop reading this and go grab some recent proposals you've submitted. Now that you've got them in your hand, be honest — are they bold, or are they bland and ordinary? Do they command your attention? Do they make you want to read them, or can you instantly tell that it will be an effort to read them?

This prospective new client is looking for a firm that is unique. There are hundreds of firms that can accomplish the work, but only one that has the unique talents and approaches of your firm. Your proposal effort is one of your prime opportunities to strut that singularity.

You're going to make your proposal a clear, proud statement that your firm is not like the rest. Never aim to be 'average' or 'adequate.' Aim to either score a perfect "10," or go down in flames and come dead last with a '0.'

The most important idea in marketing is *differentiation*.

Do you stand out in the crowd?

If every firm were identical, the services they sell would be commodities and clients would select exclusively on price.

In some ways, life would be much easier. You'd employ a room full of estimators who processed bid requests. They'd put together quotes — kind of like those Internet sites for car insurance — and you'd win some projects and lose others.

But every firm is not identical. Your firm has significant value, both basic value and added value, to bring to your clients. You pride yourself on how you do your work, the unique approaches you bring to solving your clients' challenges and the singular chemistry that defines your team.

If you're so different, why then do your business development, proposal and presentation efforts look and sound like every other firm's?

Think that yours is somehow different? Let's examine just one fragment of your sales effort. Pull out one of your recent proposals and see if you recognize some of these features:

- It's bound with a plastic comb or spiral binding.
- The title on the front cover is a direct re-statement of the project title given by the client in the RFP.
- The cover letter begins with a statement similar to: "We are pleased to have this opportunity to submit this proposal." Or, "Thank you for the opportunity to submit this proposal."
- The relevant experience and resume sections consist primarily of lists of projects you've done.
- The "Project Approach" section tells how your 'team approach' will ensure the project's success.

These aren't features taken from <u>your</u> proposal. They are features found in virtually every proposal ever written for the past 20 years! Talk about an industry stuck in a rut!

I believe that every proposal writer should be sentenced to 30 days of reviewing and evaluating other firm's proposals! It would underscore just how little difference there is between capture plans today. By and large, if you remove the names and logos from the documents, there is virtually nothing to distinguish one from another.

You, however, have just decided that differentiation is a key to your future business development efforts and you want to learn everything you can about it.

The economic definition of a 'commodity' is any product or service that, in the perception of the buyer, is essentially identical to that available from a competitor in every way except price. So a primary goal of all your marketing and sales efforts is to set your firm apart from your competitors — to give your clients a good reason (other than low price) to select you instead of them.

There are four methods that your firm can use to differentiate itself:

1. Demonstrate experience in the targeted project type. This is by far the most primitive and the least effective means of distinguishing your firm from your competition. But it's also the most common. It's the 'list of projects we've done that are similar to the current project.' But every competitor has that list. If they didn't, we wouldn't call them 'competitors.' The most challenging aspect of this technique is to show that your experience is *unique*. More often than not, the proposals I see simply say, 'we did a project like this.'

2. Show that the *process* you use to accomplish a client's goals is different and superior to that used by the competition. Today's client, concerned about quality and budget control, is sophisticated and vitally interested in the methods you use to achieve their objectives. Demonstration and explanation of your process also communicates competence and builds confidence. Letting the client see 'behind the curtain' gives them a sense of belonging to the inner circle and encourages a closer bond.

3. Prove that the value of your services is quantitatively better than those of your competition. This means measuring and demonstrating improved efficiency, economy, or

productivity for your client as a result of your work. This is the most effective and meaningful means of differentiating, but it's also the most difficult. Most other industries use this method regularly (think about the two socks, one washed in new, improved Clean-O detergent and the other in brand X) but it's virtually never done in the design industry. While it's difficult, it's not impossible. Can you show that the long-term cost of operation and maintenance of facilities you design is lower than average? That your projects are granted permits more quickly than the average? That the contractor bids on your projects are more accurate than average?

4. Let every aspect of contact with your firm be an experience that is different from that of your competitors. This includes everything from the way you answer the phone, to the way you manage projects to the way you conduct your business development and sales efforts. Your firm must look, feel, act and be different from all the others.

The bottom line of all marketing is differentiation. How is your firm different than the one across town

Client focus and customer service

Did you know that everyone in the world shares the same favorite subject? We all do — it's our own, ego-centric selves.

When you're preparing and executing a capture plan, your comfort zone lies in talking and writing about your favorite subject — your own firm. But when a client listens to and reads your proposal or your marketing message, they want to hear about *their* favorite subject. The truth is, they really aren't interested in knowing about you, except as it affects them.

As the client reads through your proposal and listens to your presentation they're asking themselves, "what's in this for me?" Yes, they want to know about your experience, but they want to know how it applies to them. What's the best way to show all the benefits that are in it for your client?

Instead of providing a simple list of what you've done, interpret for them. Tell them what you learned from the experience and how that wisdom will now save them money, reduce their schedule, or make them more popular with voters. Instead of telling them that your firm has been in business for 50 years, tell them how they benefit from a half-century of accumulated lessons-learned. Instead of telling them that you have seven offices in four states, tell them how they'll benefit from having boots on the ground in very close proximity to their project locations. I think you get the picture.

Your marketing communication must be first and foremost about your client, and it must show them *directly* how they will be better off having hired you. Don't talk about you. Talk about how that client is going to benefit from you. The difference is subtle but important.

Does social media belong in your marketing plan?

You can't turn around today without someone asking you to friend them on Facebook or follow them on Twitter. Add the LinkedIn's, Blogspot's, myspace's, flickr's, YouTube's and Pinterest's of the world and you are drowning in the social media sea, wondering if anyone will throw you a line. Let's take a quick look at social media and establish some important guidelines for your marketing and business development efforts.

First and foremost, it's vital to know that social media is not a 'strategy.' It's a tool. One of many tools that are available for you to use to implement your strategy. Like any tool, if wielded well and applied to the right job, it can work wonders. But the wrong tool, used for the wrong job can just make a mess.

Guideline #1:

Social media is one of many tools in your toolbox. Use it aggressively when the job calls for it. Otherwise, leave it at home.

Second, recognize that there is a fundamental difference between social media and 'traditional' media used for marketing and promotion. Traditional media channels such as advertising, PR, direct mail, etc., provide a one-way communication in which you send information out into the marketplace with little or no expectation of return commentary. Social media, in contrast, is a conversation. It's a two-way dialogue in which both parties intend and are invited to have equal airtime.

Take the average blog. The blog writer puts out his or her ideas, but if the blog has a healthy following, the return comments and the conversation that ensues usually far outweigh the original posting. The blogger is also expected to engage with readers and respond to the comments. While they lead the conversation, they're just one of many participants. The blogger, Tweeter, or Facebook owner is also expected to sustain the conversation with regular (weekly at the very least) postings. Without an ongoing conversation, the participants go away. It's far worse to initiate a blog or a Twitter feed, and fail to maintain it, than it is to fail to start at all.

Guideline #2:

    If you're not willing or able to maintain an active, ongoing, two-way conversation, stay away from social media. You'll accomplish far more through traditional channels.

    Third, because social media is primarily a conversation, you can think of it as a 'gathering place,' where people of like minds come to participate in the chat. A neighborhood bar is an apt metaphor where people gather to converse and benefit from one another's company.

    But not everyone is comfortable in a neighborhood bar. And not everyone is comfortable reading Twitter feeds and posting to Facebook. If the key decision makers in your target market match the demographic of those who spend a good part of their day on Twitter, then you need a strong social media presence. But if that decision maker lives in a corner office and thinks a 'friend' is someone you send Christmas cards to, they aren't likely to follow you on Twitter.

Guideline #3:

    If your target market isn't regularly Tweeting, Posting, Liking and Friending, stay away from social media. You'll accomplish far more through traditional channels.

    Social media is an exciting, dynamic and rapidly changing arena. The way it is used today is vastly different than it was a year ago and will be a year from now. Stay tuned.

The secret to a great client debrief

You've poured your heart (not to mention more than a few long nights) into the proposal only to be told you came second. At that point it's easy to walk away and leave the experience behind you. Not only is it painful to dwell on the loss, there's another urgent proposal waiting to be written.

But to walk away without touching base with the client is to leave behind a golden opportunity to build a stronger relationship, increase the quality of future proposals and drive up the odds of winning in the next round.

Even when firms do conduct debriefs, they tend to be ineffective because of the way questions are asked. The commonly asked questions — some variation on 'Please tell us how we did' — result in noncommittal answers – some variation on 'Yours was one of many good proposals; It was a tough decision; Please continue to submit on future RFPs; etc.' These give you no real feedback and provide no real guidance for your next proposal.

The secret to a good debrief is to give your client *permission* to constructively criticize. Instead of vague, open-ended questions such as 'How did we do?' ask specific questions that invite real feedback about your proposal:

- Please tell me the three things you liked most about our proposal.
- Please tell me the three things you liked least about it.
- What would you like to see changed in the next proposal we submit that might increase our chances of winning?
- What did the winning firm include in their proposal that put them over the top?
- When you think about the proposals that have won your projects in recent years, what are the common traits that made them stand out from the rest?

Questions worded in this way make it clear that you are seeking specific advice and that you won't be offended by the answers. They politely invite and give permission for criticism.

In addition to increasing the quality of future proposals, there are other real advantages to proposal debriefs conducted this way.

- The client sees that you are truly interested in improving your submittals
- You demonstrate your long-term interest in them
- You have an opportunity to further enhance your relationship and increase the odds of winning the next project.

Never pass on the opportunity to conduct a debrief after you've submitted a losing proposal. And while you're at it, why not conduct the same debrief even when you've won?

Closed Jobs Analysis

Sometimes it's difficult to tell ahead of time whether or not a project type, project size or a particular client is going to result in a profitable and successful project. But hindsight is usually 20/20 and it pays to conduct regular analysis on the projects you have completed and closed out. This process is called 'Closed Jobs Analysis' and it provides insight that can be startling.

Here's how it works. Collect the following data on ALL projects going back at least two, and preferably three or four years, and place it into a simple spreadsheet: Gross revenue, Net revenue, profit, labor hours, project type, client type, project manager.

Once you've entered the data, start sorting by the various criteria and look for patterns.

Examples from two firms will highlight how this works and the results that you can see.

Firm One conducted an analysis of all projects completed during the past three years. There were no patterns of profitability based on project type or client type, but when project size was the central variable the firm made a huge discovery. When looking at individual projects, those with total fees below $12,000 accounted for more than 35% of labor costs, but just 17% of profit. When the cutoff was raised to fees of $25,000, these accounted for almost 55% of labor but just 22% of profits.

Stated another way, if they'd cut out all the small fee projects, the firm could have worked about half the hours and still made more than 75% of the profit.

Firm Two also conducted an analysis of projects from the past three years. In their case, project size had no impact on profitability, but project type was a huge influence. With fees totaling about $2.25 million after about 18,000 labor hours, profits were around 12% at just under $270,000. But of six categories of project type, two of them, accounting for almost $350,000 in revenue and 5,000 hours of labor, did not make money on a single project. In fact they combined for a net loss of about $55,000.

The analysis showed that the vast majority of the firm's profits came from three of the six project types. If the three poor performers were eliminated completely the company's revenue would have dropped from $2.25 million to $1.3 million, labor hours would have dropped from 18,000 to less than 8,000 and profit would have INCREASED from $270,000 to more than $320,000!

Keep a "dossier" on your competitors

James Bond does it. Every large corporation does it. You, too, need to keep a close eye on your competition.

Every time Chrysler comes out with a new mini-van, the first two off the line are snapped up, one by Ford and the other by General Motors. They dismantle them, reverse-engineer the systems and features of the car and conduct in-depth analyses of the pricing strategy. Why? Because they can't survive without knowing the activities and strategies of their competitors.

Neither can you.

It's a good idea to maintain a file (let's call it a "dossier," it's so much more like James Bond!) on your main competitors. It could include a printout of their web site, a copy of their brochure, a list of principals and key employees with outline resumes and any other pertinent information about key clients, project histories and known strengths and weaknesses.

Gathering this information isn't hard. Between the Internet, your clients, contractors and sub-consultants and even former employees who might now be working for you, there is lots of information available. Start asking and digging and you'll be amazed at what you can find!

What should you do with the information you gather?

In the long term you need to maintain strong differentiation in the market. If other firms are looking more and more like you everyday, it may be complimentary but it's bad for business. Many of your strategic planning decisions will be based on opportunities and threats that exist in the marketplace. A competitor that is coming on strong is a decided threat.

In the short term this information can help you get more closely "wired" to your clients. Let's say you're going up against a certain competitor on a new water treatment plant project for a local municipality. Your research tells you that one of your main competitors has recently given a seminar at the regional APWA (American Public Works Association) conference and was very well received. This could give them a strong advantage since the local Public Works Director would be impressed with their obvious expertise. With this knowledge you could:

- Mount an extra effort to build on your personal relationship with the Public Works Director
- Conduct a short, direct mail program in which you send a series of tips on state-of-the-art treatment plant maintenance and technology to the ten Public Works Directors within a 50-mile radius.
- Investigate pursuing the project as a joint venture with the competitor.
- Connect with a nationally-known consultant who has presented an even more impressive seminar.

There may be other strategies you can implement but the point is that each of these strategies acknowledges the reality of the marketplace. Without this information you would walk in blind and then wonder why the other firm won

Timeless wisdom

I was going through some old files and came across a memo that had been written more than 30 years ago. The author was a design firm Principal who had just "sat on the other side of the table." In other words, he had just experienced what it's like to be a client trying to select a design firm. His advice and encouragement to the other members of his firm is as good and on-target as it gets.

I spent all day yesterday listening to four joint venture firms give presentations for their services. It drilled home once again that good business development is essential if we are to sell work. In the Olympics there might be 18 inches' difference between first and last place runners; and all the losers could easily win races elsewhere.

We are up against increasingly stiff competition. We're competing against people who really understand good marketing techniques, good sales, and good presentations. We've got to be outstanding to close that last 18 inches.

Here are some thoughts that occurred to me yesterday. We've discussed them all in the past, but I wanted to re-emphasize them to you.

1.   Make sure we understand what the client wants.
You can't find that by reading the RFP. You've got to talk to the people who are doing the hiring. I was surprised yesterday at how few people talked to me or the other members of the interview committee before the interview. We were all available for questions.

2.   Include the buyer benefits.
Most of the presenters told us what they were going to do. But they didn't emphasize what the benefit to us would be. Sometimes we were able to infer the benefit; sometimes we couldn't. A few of the better presenters described their services in simple, declarative sentences, and then explained the benefits that would accrue to us if we hired them to provide those services.

3.   *Prepare and rehearse*
     It was clear that some of the firms had spent time preparing for us, and some of them had not. The ones that prepared were well organized. They addressed important points with simple, declarative sentences, and they seemed relaxed and unconfused. The ones that hadn't prepared and rehearsed stumbled all over themselves, corrected one another and missed the mark.

4.   *Don't talk about yourself too much.*
     Several of the companies failed miserably because they just told us all about themselves and what they had done. We'd already read all about that in their proposals. What we wanted to know was how they were going to do our job. The companies that came out on top were the ones that spent all their time talking about how they were going to do things for us.

5.   *Excitement and innovation sure help.*
     The firms that came out on top were those that clearly were excited by the opportunity, and had innovative approaches. It was clear who had thought the job through and who came in with their canned "we're big and this is the way we do it" approach. The companies that sold their traditional services failed. Those that met the unique needs of the project succeeded.

I couldn't have said it better myself.

So you're in it for the money

There is no reason why you shouldn't make a lot of money in the engineering and architecture business. But maybe no one's ever told you how. There are four steps to making money in this business:

Step 1:
Sell something that can't be bought on just any street corner
    Why? Because in the minds of your customers "great engineering" can be purchased from a thousand sources. What's the difference between the pump you specify and the one your competitor does? Do you use a different formula to calculate the loads on your structures?

    The bad news is, engineering is a very mature industry. There are way too many competitors and the services they sell are commodities — the only difference between buying from one firm or another is the price.

    Don't get me wrong, there is nothing wrong with selling commodities. It's a perfectly viable business model. Just ask Wal-Mart. The secret to success is to cut costs, then cut them some more and sell in high volume. One day, someone is going to open *"Tony's Super Engineering Discount Warehouse Direct!" "We're open Sunday's till midnight and we won't be undersold!"*

    If you don't want to compete against Tony, you'd better make sure the services you sell are unique or 'packaged' in a way that is appealing, convenient or new to your customers. Frankly, there is very little to offer in engineering that is truly unique. 'Unparalleled customer service' offers a whole world of possibilities, but our industry hasn't even begun to scratch that surface. Targeting particular niche markets or providing rare technical expertise also qualifies as 'unique' but most of your opportunities lie in 're-packaging' the services you already offer.

Design/build is simply re-packaging. So are Construction Management and Program Management. Performance contracting, bundled services that include financing and engineering, commissioning, and facilities management are also innovative ways to polish up traditional services so they look new.

If you're scoffing at what you see as window dressing, check the profit margins of the firms that have replaced "Engineering" with some of these other words on the sign above their door.

Step 2:
Market like hell

"Build a better mousetrap and the world will beat a path to your door." There has never been a more blatant lie. If the world hasn't heard about your mousetrap, how on earth are they going to find your door?

If you want to make money, you've got to make noise. Lots of noise. Get out in the community. Join client-rich organizations. Speak from the podium and write for the journals. Shake lots of hands. Get your name in the paper. Learn how to use direct mail. Learn how to use public relations.

The world's wealthiest people are also the world's best self-promoters. In contrast, most design firms are rank amateurs when it comes to marketing. They blow the opportunity to build name recognition and 'mind share' by seeing marketing as a cost, instead of an investment.

Become a student of marketing. Learn its subtleties and how you can use them to advantage. The most profitable firms are spending in excess of 10% of net revenue on aggressive, proactive marketing.

So far, pretty simple, huh?

Step 3:
Use profit-oriented pricing strategies

What is the highest hourly rate your firm can ever charge? $150 per hour? $200 per hour? $350 per hour!? Let's say it's up there in the stratosphere at $350 per hour. Taken at face value, that means there is absolutely nothing you or anyone in your firm can accomplish in one hour's time that is worth more than $350.

What nonsense!

Hourly fees, and especially hourly fees with a not-to-exceed cap, are absurd for a design firm. They doom you to subsistence-level survival and they completely discount the value you bring. The most profitable firms focus on clients and markets that can be priced on value, not cost. They turn down work that doesn't allow them to make a high profit and they position themselves by proactively educating their target markets about the value they add.

How often have you sat in a one-hour meeting with a permitting agency and negotiated a concession on behalf of a client that saved that client $10,000 in project costs? What did you charge the client for that one-hour meeting?

You can't make money selling hours by the pound.

Step 4:
Keep what you make

On average, engineering firms leave somewhere between 25% and 50% of the fees they are paid sitting on the table. How do they manage this remarkable feat?

- Poor project planning
- Working outside the paid scope
- Lack of inter-discipline coordination
- Lackluster negotiation skills
- Over-designing

The list goes on. And on.

Poor project management is like a giant hole in the bottom of your bank account. The money just pours right through. Sure, you've got a project management manual. But do people actually use it? Consistently? What are the consequences to an employee who prefers to do things his or her own way? Are your project managers really trained? What qualified them to be project managers in the first place?

There isn't an engineering firm in business today that couldn't increase profits by 50% with a little effort towards improving the way projects are managed. If you really set your mind to it, you could probably raise profits by 100% or more.

What could you do with that money?

Your design firm should be wonderfully profitable. The fact that it isn't is not the fault of your clients, your competitors, the government or aliens. It's your fault. If you'd like to do something about it, why not start today?

Why your attempts to use CRM aren't working

(Hint: it isn't the software)

One of the goals I want to achieve before I pass on to a better world is to learn to play the piano. I have a small electronic keyboard on which I am capable of making nasty plunking sounds that, if you really listen carefully, might sound like 'Mary Had a Little Lamb.' Needless to say, I'm not yet satisfied with my performance. But I have a plan: I'm going to spend $100,000 to buy a Steinway grand piano because with this far superior instrument, I'm sure I'll be able to make beautiful music.

Many firms that are experiencing less than stellar results as they try to implement a Customer Relationship Management (CRM) system are attempting the same kind of fruitless approach. 'If we just buy a more sophisticated software package, then our CRM will work.'

'Fraid not.

Like learning to play the piano, learning to properly implement CRM has little to do with the instrument and a lot to do with the student. The challenge is not one of choosing the right software, the challenge is changing the culture of your organization to one that embraces the selling process. Once that happens, everyone will recognize the tremendous value that a CRM system can provide and happily participate.

The point of failure that most firms attempting to implement CRM are experiencing is in getting the individuals involved in business development to record details of the ongoing conversation with prospective clients. It takes too long. It's too much trouble. I've got too much project work to do. I forgot... There are dozens of handy excuses but they all add up to failure.

Some firms have even developed a work-around in which the business developer will make or dictate notes that are then handed to a secretary or assistant who enters them in 'the system.' This is rather like buying a Ferrari and pulling it around with a horse.

Too many design firms view the sale as a point in time that signals the beginning of a project. But every great sales organization understands that a sale isn't an event, it's a process that needs to be tracked and managed. In the same way that a project is a long series of tasks that must be carefully managed, business development, client management and sales are elements in a process that require careful management. CRM is a tool to help manage that process and if a firm lacks a culture that embraces the sales process, it won't be successful with CRM. If you can't make it work with index cards and a shoebox, you can't make it work with fancy software.

Spending big bucks for the most elaborate CRM software is a waste of money because the existing culture will doom it to failure. The best way to implement CRM is to start on a pilot project basis. Let a few of the early-adopters — those who understand how sales really works — work with it for six months. Evaluate the results and make any necessary tweaks to the system. Then expand usage to the next most likely group. Have at least a year of successful implementation, lessons-learned, successful users, evangelists and in-house coaches before you eventually incorporate everyone.

When does your Loss-Free Day occur?

(You have to pay taxes, but you don't have to pay for this)

We all love paying our taxes and as a God-fearing, law-abiding and tax-paying citizen, you've no doubt heard about Tax-Free Day. That's the first day in the year when you stop working for the government and start working for yourself. Until that morning dawns, every buck you earn goes to paying federal and state income taxes, county and city taxes, sales and use taxes, social security contributions and all the other energy, sin, and just-because-we-can taxes.

Tax-free day falls on a different day based on where you live, what you earn and the color of your first-born's eyes, and there's little or nothing you can do about it.

Now let's talk about Loss-Free Day.

Haven't heard of this one? That's the day of the year when you stop paying for all the profit fade your company endures as a result of poor project management and margin begins to stick to your own bottom line. Each time a project manager allows scope to creep or a designer wants to explore just one more option, Loss-Free Day gets pushed further into the year.

Whenever you agree to take a job that your go/no-go checklist suggests you should ignore, there is one less day in the year to pocket profit. Every day you go home with an outstanding receivable sitting in someone else's bank account, your Loss-Free Day slips again.

There's a big difference between Tax Free and Loss-Free Day: You're stuck with taxes, but don't have to put up with project losses.

Calculating your Loss-Free Day is easy, and it can be done company-wide or for an individual project. The formula works like this:

$$\frac{\text{Budgeted margin} - \text{actual margin}}{\text{Budgeted margin}} \times 365$$

Let's say your $10 million engineering company budgets a net profit before taxes for the year of $1.2 million. Instead, at the end of the year, net profit ends up at $950,000. In this case, your Loss-Free Day would be:

$$\frac{\$1,200,000 - \$950,000 \quad x \quad 365}{\$1,200,000} = 76$$

That puts Loss-Free Day 76 days into the year, on March 17.

Let's take a nine-month engineering design project with revenue of $250,000 and a budgeted profit of $37,500. When the job's done it turns out that profit has eroded to just $21,500. In this case, the Loss-Free Day would be:

$$\frac{\$37,500 - \$21,500 \quad x \quad 365}{\$37,500} = 156$$

Loss-Free Day for this project would be June 5th.

Hurts, doesn't it?

High awareness of and motivation towards front-end loading, tight scope control, high productivity and early collections can make January 1st your firm's Loss-Free Day. Effective negotiations and careful change-order management can even turn your Loss-Free Day into a negative number. That means this year's profits began accumulating last year!

Publishing loss-free day as one of your key performance indicators and providing effective tools, processes, and training to your project managers, technical teams and accounting staff can light a real fire and keep everyone focused on protecting that precious margin.

The story of the $1 million fee

A few years back I was asked to help a firm chase a particular project. They wanted it badly because it came with a $1 million fee and they'd never won a project that big before. The principals were drooling all over themselves and planning how they would spend every one of those million dollars.

A year before they'd been awarded a small feasibility study. While the study didn't pay big bucks, it preceded the larger project and the plan was to use the feasibility study as a marketing opportunity to win the big prize. They pulled out all the stops and did a better job than anyone had expected. The results were fabulous and the client was thrilled.

But...

The fee for the study was $15,000. The firm's cost for this study-to-end-all-studies was $60,000.

I pointed out that they were now $45,000 in the hole. "Of course," they replied, "but what's $45,000 compared to a $1 million fee?"

I then asked about the status of the project. Was it real? Did the client have the money to build it? They said that everything was in place with one small exception — the bond issue had yet to be passed.

Now a bond issue is a very big deal. It's tied up by politics, personalities, the mood of the voters and quite possibly the phase of the moon. There was a reasonable chance it would not get passed and the project would die on the vine. My client estimated the chances of the bond passing to be 50/50.

Then we looked at another potential deal buster — the competition. "Is the project," I asked, "wired for you? Is it yours if the bond is passed?" Apparently there was still one other firm in the running, but since my client had done the feasibility study, they felt the chances of winning were very good. I asked what their estimate of the odds of beating this competitor was and they guessed them to be 70/30.

Basic math shows that if you combine the two odds (50% chance of passing the bond and 70% of beating the competition) the overall chance of having the project land in the door is now down to 35%. I pointed this out and, not having looked at the project this way before, their faces grew a little pale.

The topic then switched to profitability. The firm was not terribly efficient and consistently made a profit of eight or nine percent on their projects. But this one was a little out of the ordinary and would require a learning curve. They estimated the profit they would be able to make on the project to be five percent.

Basic math again shows five percent of $1 million to be $50,000. Subtract from this the $45,000 that was invested in the marketing and (ignoring financing, other marketing expenses, or costly mistakes) the net profit from the project would be $5,000.

Their faces became a little paler still.

Here was the situation they faced:

- They had put a $45,000 bet on a horse.
- The horse had a 3.5 in 10 chance of winning the race.
- There was no payout for second or third place as there is in a horse race. In this race you either win, or you lose.
- If their horse did win, it would pay out a mere $5,000.

It always gets your heart beating a little faster as you take part in 'the chase.' But keep in mind that you are in business to stay in business and prosper, not to write proposals. Your Go/No Go procedure weeds out 'opportunities' that are trouble in the making. And, if you go through the analysis and decide to pursue the project anyway, at least you'll be walking in with your eyes open, ready for surprises.

The end of the story?

Sometimes fairy tales do come true. The bond passed and the firm was successful with the project.

Avoiding the Trite Trap

Having read hundreds of design firm proposals over the last several decades, I have concluded that much of what is presented as valuable content is, in fact, trite and meaningless rubbish.

Sound harsh? To add some science to this otherwise gut-level conclusion, I've developed what I call the "Trite Test." It can be applied to any communication, written or verbal, that you send to a prospective client in hopes that he or she will hire you.

Here's how it works:

Since the bottom line of all marketing is differentiation, i.e., 'what have you got that the other guy doesn't," it's reasonable that any marketing statement you make should further distinguish you from them. To apply the Trite Test, ask this question:

> *"Could I imagine one of my competitors, in an effort to differentiate himself from me, saying the opposite of what I've just said?"*

Let's try an example; a tired, worn-out statement used in a proposal cover letter.

> *"Acme Engineers is pleased to submit this proposal."*

Apply the Trite Test and imagine someone writing, *"We're really annoyed at having to prepare and submit this proposal."* Of course not! The fact that you were pleased to submit is self-evident. If you had not been pleased you wouldn't have bothered. So it's a corny statement that adds nothing to your submission.

When you realize that every cover letter of every proposal begins with that same sentence (or a subtle variation of it), it becomes even more clichéd and meaningless. Worse, instead of setting you apart, it only reinforces the perception that your firm is just like everyone else who has submitted.

Here are some more hackneyed statements that appear in proposals in one form or another.

> *"We are uniquely qualified."*

While this may be true, the statement by itself proves nothing. Instead of using this stale and ever-present assertion, get specific and cite examples of your unique qualifications: *"Our unique scheduling process will ensure the smooth operation of the rest of your facility during construction."*

"Our firm has been in business for XX years."

If a firm is more than 25 years old, all the old guys are either retired or dead and no one is getting the benefit of their experience. Besides, experience gained on projects more than 15 years old is irrelevant today. The client did not set out to hire a firm with a specific number of years' experience. They want a firm that can solve today's problem regardless of how long it's been in business. Don't talk about years of experience, talk about the lessons you've learned, captured and shared. Relate a case study of a lesson-learned that was applied to another project and how that client benefited. The statement that your firm has been in business 100 years could easily be interpreted to mean that it's just old and tired!

"We will meet your schedule and budget."

Imagine going to buy a new car and having the salesman tell you that you should buy this car because "It will start every morning!" Reliability like that became available long ago and we've moved on to much higher expectations. Clients today fully expect that you will meet schedule and budget — that's merely the ante into the game. Instead, show how you're going to go above and beyond the minimum requirement.

Trite clichés do nothing to inspire a client to prefer your firm over another. Instead, they strongly reinforce the impression that yours is just like all the others. Ask a trusted client if you can borrow some old proposals they've received from other firms. Review them and see for yourself just how much they sound like yours. Then purge all the tired, commonplace and unoriginal statements from your marketing and sales efforts so you can truly stand apart from the crowd.

So what?

The company had asked me to conduct a training seminar on presentation skills and we had spent the better part of the day with the video camera, recording design professionals laboring through the slides, boards and scripts of their most recent interviews. Without fail, each time someone got up to speak, they turned their back on the audience and watched as slide after slide of past projects shot onto the screen.

I patiently reminded them that they needed to let the audience know why they should look at a particular slide and what benefit they could expect to gain from that knowledge. But, as the afternoon wore on, it was obvious that I wasn't getting through.

In desperation I pulled out a big fat marker and wrote "So What?" on a piece of paper. Every time someone would say, "And here's another project we've done..." I would hold up the sign and force them to explain the relevance of the project they were showing to the one at hand. It was a painful process and I wasn't sure the lesson was really sinking in. So we decided to raise the stakes.

The company had a project interview coming up the following week and I made them a dare. I dared them to invite the client selection panel to use the "So What?" signs.

They were in the mood for risk taking so we used the laser printer to prepare some professional-looking signs and mounted them on popsicle-stick handles. (How professional can a sign that says, "So What?" be?)

As the presentation team introduced themselves at the interview they handed one sign to each member of the review panel. They instructed the panel that, if at any time during the interview they felt their time was being wasted or the team was talking about things that didn't seem relevant to them, they were to hold up their signs.

The client thought this was a little odd, but the novelty intrigued them and they had sat through too many lifeless interviews to object.

It wasn't long before the old habits started to surface. One of the presenters slipped comfortably into his old routine of showing off his slide collection with his back to the audience. But this time, someone held up his "So What?" sign.

At that point the presenter stopped, thanked the client for helping him improve the quality of his presentation, and pointed out that the construction techniques used in the project shown in the slide were going to be used to solve a very similar problem on the current project.

From that point on the interview was completely changed. Every time someone put up a "So What?" sign, which quickly become a fun game for the client, not only did everyone have a good laugh, the stuffy monologue was converted to a high-energy dialogue. There was an electric exchange of ideas, and the client and the firm kicked off a dynamite relationship.

When the interview was over, the firm was handed the project on the spot. In the client's words, "Anyone who has the nerve to come in here with signs like this is the kind of company we want to work with." But they had one condition: they had to keep the "So What?" signs because, "We attend plenty of meetings where these signs would be invaluable!"

Keeping clients for life

You've heard it many times before — landing a new client can cost 10, 25, 100 times more than keeping an old one. No one agrees on the actual multiple but everyone agrees that it's MUCH more expensive. And losing a client costs you all the overhead and marketing you've invested in landing them in the first place. So keeping your clients happy in a long-term relationship is just good business — higher profits, lower overheads, less stress and the peace of mind of a steady supply of profitable work.

In these days of intense competition, your clients are taking some very hard looks at why they are continuing to work with the same consultants and suppliers and whether or not they should switch. It takes a lot more than loyalty to keep a client today!

Let's look at six practices you can adopt to ensure your clients stay around and continue to come back to you for project after project. It might be worthwhile to have both your marketing team and your project managers read this article, since the responsibility for keeping clients for life lies squarely on their shoulders.

1.   Provide over-the-top customer service

Every one of your competitors can produce the same great technical work that you can. That's why we call them 'competitors!' So why should a client choose to hire you instead of them? Over-the-top customer service will give you a competitive edge that technical expertise and even low price can never overcome. You've experienced great customer service (just not often enough) and you know that you're willing to pay extra for it.

Imagine for a minute that you own and operate a store. But instead of clothes or groceries, your store sells engineering. What is it like to shop at your store? What do customers experience when they come in? How are they greeted? Are they made to feel wanted and welcome? How are they treated by the staff? What are they thinking when they leave?

What can you do to improve that experience and make it more pleasant and memorable?

2. Seek regular feedback

The idea of seeking out regular, reliable and candid feedback from clients is simultaneously exciting and terrifying. It feels great to get the 'attaboys' and the glowing testimonials when things go well, but what kind of feedback do you want or get when you screw up? How often do you actively seek your clients' opinions about what you do well and what you do poorly? More importantly, what do you do with those opinions when they're given?

The first lesson in looking for client feedback is a word of caution. Regardless of how you learn what clients think about your firm, once they've shared their thoughts they fully expect you're going to do something about it. If you're not prepared to act on the suggestions and make real changes based on the feedback you receive, don't ask for it. Soliciting opinions and then doing nothing is far worse than failing to ask in the first place. If they had some concerns before, they're really annoyed now.

"We'll exceed your expectations" is a cornball statement that fools no one... unless you can back it up by describing your firm's program to determine, measure and track client expectations and your action plan to respond to them. Set your firm apart from everyone else by telling your client how your process includes regular client feedback and maybe even a meeting specifically designed to identify and quantify their project expectations from which your team will establish goals and procedures to go beyond those goals by a measurable ten percent.

Now that's impressive.

3. Admit when you're wrong

First, apologize. None of us particularly likes being caught at our less-than-best. But letting your clients and colleagues see the less perfect side of you shows you to be real. It's especially important when you mess up (and who doesn't mess up periodically?) to 'fess up and admit your mistake. This gives you a credibility that you can never achieve by always claiming to be right or infallible. If they see that you're honest as you deal with mistakes, they will assume that you are honest in all your dealings.

Second, make it right. We all make mistakes. It's what you do after the mistake that separates the good from the great. While swallowing the big pill of remedying a mistake may seem tough at the time, the long-term cost of not stepping up and doing the right thing is much greater. Compare the difference in public perception on two huge oil spills. After the Exxon Valdez incident, the company tried to deny wrongdoing and dodge responsibility, which resulted in a huge public relations mess. In contrast, when BP stepped in following the explosion in the Gulf of Mexico, we all criticized the original mistake, but gave the company full marks for their response.

4.   Be price sensitive

Times are always challenging and we all have to watch our budgets. While no one is asking you to slash your prices, be sensitive to your client's situation and be willing to take a smaller margin in order to help your client go ahead with the project. Can you defer some scope items on a project until later so that they're able to go ahead with the project now?

Or why not take a lesson from the airlines? Do your frequent and loyal customers receive any type of discount on the price of their work? Can they earn 'points' that can be redeemed later on for an additional scope item or a small study? Loyalty programs are popular in many industries because they reward and lock-in customer allegiance. Since you're saving money on marketing with repeat customers, why not refund some of those savings in return for their loyalty?

5.   Give back

Way back in kindergarten we all learned that, in order to receive, we have to be willing to give. In the adult world, we look for ways to give back to our friends and families, our communities, our alma maters and the environment.

Business development is all about looking for and asking for work. Relationships, on the other hand, are a two-way street that gives as well as receives. So before you ask your clients for another project, ask yourself what you've given to them lately.

Do you have information on market trends that might be valuable? Do you have knowledge about new technologies or processes that they would find useful? Do you have a dozen donuts that they might enjoy?

6. *Show your appreciation regularly*

You can never say 'thank you' too many times. Your clients aren't just the source of your livelihood. Most of us enjoy friendships, professional relationships, mentoring and plain old good times with many of our clients. Make sure you express your gratitude for the friendships you enjoy, the assistance and guidance you are given, the revenue you depend on and the sustainability of your business because of the people with whom you work.

Your mother was right: don't forget to say 'thank you.'

The project that wasn't there

I was asked to give a proposal-writing workshop to a firm on the West Coast. I suggested that they would get the most from the workshop if we could work with an actual RFP to which they were going to respond. We could spend the day actually writing the proposal.

When I arrived at eight o'clock that morning, the RFP was sitting on the table. I assumed they had some background so we began the discussion by me asking questions about the project.

> *"Who is this client?"*
> *"It's a municipality about 20 miles away."*
> *"Have we worked for them before?"*
> *"No."*
> *"Then how did we get the RFP?"*
> *"It came in the mail."*
> *"But how did this client decide to send it to us?"*
> *"We don't know."*
> *"How did this client get our name?"*
> *"We don't know."*
> *"Who else has been asked to respond?"*
> *"We don't know."*

By this time it was obvious the firm knew little or nothing about the client, the project, the selection process or the competition. But, as often happens, they were about to spend almost $5,000 to prepare and submit a proposal that would be nothing more than a shot in the dark. I could not go along with it.

I called for a break and went off with the marketing coordinator and a secretary to play a game I call 'Scavenger Hunt.' They were each given a phone, the Internet and 20 minutes. Their assignment: find out anything and everything about this project. They began dialing.

20 minutes later they had find out that:

- The client, a municipality about 20 miles away, was merely "thinking about" doing the project.
- The project was only a dream and no funding was in place.

- The RFP was simply intended to 'kick some tires' and obtain feedback on costs to determine if they would actually be able to do the project.
- The firm was one of twelve who had been invited to submit proposals.
- The client had been given the firm's name by a sub-consultant who had also submitted the names of four other prime consultants. (Thank you very much!)

In short, they found out enough in 20 minutes to decide without hesitation that the project did not warrant the effort and expense of a proposal. We reconvened and drafted a short letter of regret to the client.

The punch line to this story is that the firm's principals then told me they were glad we decided not to pursue the project because now we had time to work on another, really important proposal they had to prepare!

Making a great first impression

Scary story # 1:

Some years ago I was facilitating a proposal-writing workshop with about 20 CEOs of design firms. I had a stack of real proposals and I asked the group to think of themselves as a client selection panel. Their job was to review the proposals and reduce the large pile to two smaller ones: the short list and the rejects.

We passed out the proposals and these high-ranking executives dove into them. What these CEOs didn't know was that I was timing how long they took to make that initial decision about 'Pile A' or 'Pile B.' The average time spent with each proposal before making that initial, crucial decision was 18 seconds.

18 seconds! It takes longer than that to brush your teeth! And yet these highly skilled executives were willing to make important decisions based on the information they could assimilate in that incredibly short time.

Scary story # 2:

More recently I had occasion to be at the NAVFAC (Naval Facilities Command) in Norfolk, VA where I was meeting with one of the Navy's Contracting Officers. She related how, in response to an RFP, she had received 50 proposals. Lacking the time to review them all she instructed her assistant to line all the proposals up, leaning on the marker ledge below the white boards in the conference room. She then proceeded to walk into the room and, from a distance of 10 feet, select the 12 proposals she would review in detail.

On what were the executives and the contracting officer making the decisions? Nothing more than first impressions! As a result, I determined that the first and most important section of any proposal is the section we'll call First Impressions. It impacts the critical first 20 seconds in which your client lays eyes on your proposal document and can put you on, or keep you off the short list.

When seeing your proposal for the first time, how does your client react? Are they impressed and intrigued? Are they motivated to open and read it? Are they inclined to give you credibility and advantage? Or are they bored and disinterested because it looks and feels just like the last five proposals they've just reviewed?

The "First Impressions" section is intended to make an instant and significant impact and consists of:

- The cover and binding
- The title you've given the document
- The page layout, paper, and fonts you've used
- The cover letter you have written

These important elements need to grab that reviewer's attention and intrigue them enough to spend more time with your proposal. Because they don't have the time or the motivation to read every word you've written and find that vital information that's half way down page 17.

Here are some specific ways you can get your proposal to jump out of the pile and make a fabulous first impression.

An Intriguing Cover Story
A little imagination can go a long way

The cover of your proposal is like the packaging a retailer uses to market their products. Think about the three different shopping bags you get shopping at Wal-Mart, Macy's, and Saks Fifth Avenue. Each bag tells a very different story about the store, the quality of the products it sells, and the type of customer it hopes to attract.

You never hear Saks' customers complaining about the cost of the fancy shopping bag or the salary of the uniformed doorman as they pull up on Rodeo Drive. Nor do you hear Wal-Mart customers asking to have a doorman or more up-scale store fixtures. They know these costs would add to the overhead of the store and passed on to them.

I once saw a proposal submitted to a developer in Chicago by a design/build team. The project was a very high-end condominium project — the sort for which you pay $3 million for a studio unit. The proposal document was hardbound in black leather with gold leaf lettering on the front cover! It even smelled rich! Any client, picking up that document would immediately know that the team had completely understood the nature of the project.

Don't get me wrong. The Public Works Director reviewing your proposal to conduct smoke tests on his sanitary sewer system would not appreciate the leather and your binding choices there would be different. The point is that you DO have choices. Not every proposal should be bound with black plastic GBC comb bindings. Make the appropriate choice based on what you know of the client and the project from your research, your brainstorming and your game plan.

An Eye-Catching Title

The titles of most proposals are as dull as grey paint. Why not jazz things up a little? A good title is like a headline in a newspaper article, it grabs your attention and hints at what you can expect to discover.

If schedule is going to be a big deal on your project, refer to on-time delivery in the title. If there is a significant technical challenge on the project, work your solution into the title and splash it on the cover. Here are some examples based on an actual RFP for A/E services for a Federal correctional facility. The RFP from the client was titled:

Request for Proposal for Architect/Engineering Services
Federal Correctional Facilities
SOL RFP X00-0264
Federal Bureau of Prisons

The predictable, traditional reaction would be to title the proposal:

Response to Request for Proposal for Architect/Engineering Services
Federal Correctional Facilities
SOL RFP X00-0264
Federal Bureau of Prisons

Not only is this boring and unimaginative, it fails to tell the client anything they don't already know. It doesn't reflect any of the unique aspects of your firm and it doesn't respond to any of the issues that the project may face. Lastly, it fails to differentiate you from any competitor because you can guarantee they will all use the same title. Surely we can do better than this.

Using the 'headline' idea, if a major hot button on the project is schedule, why not try:

"Federal Prison Locked Up in 28 Months"

If the big challenge is cost control you could use:
"Under Lock, Key, and Budget"

If relations with the local community are a big issue:
"Federal Correctional Facilities: Building Community Ties"

Titles like these not only set you apart from everyone else, they intrigue and delight the reader. They give some hint about the contents of the proposal and they cause the client to forget about their 18-second clock!

A Unique Cover Letter
It doesn't always have to be 'Yours Truly...'

Your cover letter can significantly influence your client's initial reaction to your proposal. It's one of the first items the client reads in the crucial early seconds of their review and it plays an important role in forming their first impressions.

Most firms treat it as a simple transmittal letter and fill it with trite, meaningless statements such as "we are pleased to submit this proposal," or "we are uniquely qualified," and "if you have any questions, please call." These sentences appear in virtually every proposal and only reinforce the client's impression that all firms are the same. In contrast, your objective should be to do everything possible to underscore the differences between you and everyone else.

Your cover letter ought to be so powerful that your client could make up his or her mind by reading it alone. It needs to be comprehensive enough to put you on the short list but short enough to be quickly scanned and understood.

Here's how to do it. Let's say you are proposing design services for a new medical center and you've determined that there are a number of key issues that need to be addressed. These include:

1. Completing the project within 18 months
2. Maintaining positive community relations
3. Control over a very tight budget
4. Working with the input of the Board and doctors
5. You have no previous experience with this client

Using these "hot buttons" as an outline, your cover letter can address the project and the client's specific issues like this:

Dr. John Black
Western Medical Center
123 State Street
Yourtown, ST 12345

Re: Strong staff and community relations on the project

Dear Dr. Black,

The Western Medical Center's new Pediatric project provides a wonderful opportunity for the hospital to reinforce its strong community ties and staff relationships. By emphasizing the input of your Board and doctors, we fully expect that your aggressive 18-month schedule can be met within budget.

Smith and Jones has been studying this project extensively and has developed a unique scheduling process that will ensure the smooth operation of the rest of your facility during construction. To make the process as smooth as

possible we have already mapped out a schedule of community information meetings to invite comments from the surrounding neighborhood.
In addition, you can look forward to:

- *A thoughtful and coordinated process for input by Board and staff members (see page 12)*
- *A project manager with a remarkable talent for smooth community relations (page 8)*
- *A peaceful night's sleep with the knowledge that budget is well under control (see page 4)*

Although you have not had the opportunity to work with Smith and Jones previously, many of your peers have found the experience economical, efficient, professional, and downright pleasant! We invite you to review their comments that can be found throughout this proposal. In addition, working with Smith & Jones on this project will give you the opportunity to compare the levels of service, responsiveness, quality, and economy you have received from other firms.

I will contact you during the next week to clarify any questions you may have regarding our approach to the project. In the meantime, we are continuing to review the specifics of this project and prepare for kickoff.

Yours frugally,
Smith and Jones, Inc.

John J. Jones

PS   We are looking forward to demonstrating our unique cost control process at the interview.

This entire letter was built around the important client issues and avoids those 'mom-and-apple-pie' statements used by everyone else.

You'll also notice some other techniques:

- Giving each bullet point a page reference allows a reader intrigued by that issue to go straight to the relevant page.
- Using the signatory line to touch another hot button. It doesn't always have to be 'Yours Truly.'
- The "PS" is guaranteed to be read. Even if they skim your letter, they will always stop and read it. Use it to hit another hot button.

It's not surprising that the majority of selection committee participants admit they have significantly made up their minds shortly after picking up a proposal. It is in your best interest to make the most of this opportunity by making a memorable first impression.

Are you running a country club?

A few years ago I was working with an engineering firm in the Midwest and the CEO asked me to spend a couple of days poking around and assessing the organization. We had dinner together on the second night and he asked me what I'd observed.

This guy's a straight shooter so I told him outright: "You don't have a business. You have a country club." Of course he wanted a little backup on such a provocative claim, so I elaborated.

A country club is a place where you join up and are given a loose set of rules and regulations with which you're expected to comply. Don't wear your golf cleats in the dining room, don't spit on the floor... that sort of thing. But within those rules you're pretty much free to do whatever you want.

Feel like going to the gym and working with the personal trainer today? Great! Here's your towel. Had a hard day at the office and just want to sit in the lounge, read The Times and sip brandy? Terrific! That's why we have those comfortable leather armchairs. And there are no consequences for your choices. No one is going to rescind your membership if you don't work out five times a week.

And this is why his firm was like a country club: Feel like putting together a tight schedule and budget and working hard to maintain it so we make a profit? Wonderful! Here are the tools you can use to help with that. Finding our reporting system a little too challenging? That's OK, use the system you're familiar with from your previous firm and you'll still get your paycheck. And a bonus. Feel that it's a little too much trouble to enter your activities into our CRM system? No problem, we'll just limp along with whatever you can do.

And there are no consequences.

I asked the CEO what it took (short of a felony) to get fired from his firm and he genuinely didn't know!

Now imagine that you are a banker. You've just been hired as the branch manager for a new bank and this is your first day. You're toured around the bank and informed that you will be expected to open a certain number of new accounts each month. You reply that you'll try, but can't guarantee any results. You're told that you have a quota for writing new loans each quarter. That number seems a little high and you tell them so. Your District Manager tells you that he requires the monthly reports in this particular format by the 21st of each month. And you tell him that you much prefer the report format that you used at your previous bank.

Guess what! You wouldn't make it to lunch on that first day! Because banks don't run country clubs. They run businesses. Highly profitable businesses!

So look around your firm. Do you have business development expectations for your Project Managers? How many are meeting them? Do you have CRM reporting requirements? How many are complying with them? Do you have project management procedures in place? How many are using them?

Then ask yourself if you're running a business or a country club.

Let's talk about commodities

There is no end of wailing and gnashing of teeth when it comes to pricing professional design services. I bumped into it again a couple of weeks ago when a firm I was working with lost out on a project because their fee was about 80% higher than the next firm. Why aren't clients smart enough to see value?

It's not the client's job to see value. It's our job to show it and to provide higher value that is worth a higher price. And we're not doing a very good job of that.

A company selling a product or service that isn't commonly available can not only charge significantly more, they can afford to provide their customers with a level of personal attention that isn't feasible at low profit margins. When you stay at the Ritz Carlton, you get a 'free' doorman and 'free' turn-down service with exotic chocolates left on your pillow. The BMW dealer offers 'free' oil changes and scheduled maintenance as well as a 'free' car wash whenever your car is in for service.

We're all smart enough to know that none of these frills are actually free. But the increased attention and coddling are seen as value that is added to the core product or service. Let's face it, when the lights are out and you're fast asleep (the basic reason you stay at a hotel), it's hard to tell the difference between the Ritz Carlton and Motel 6.

As desirable as those value-added services might be, selling a commodity service is a perfectly viable business model. When Sam Walton died, he was the richest man in America, and he became so by learning how to sell commodities. The only 'secret' is low pricing combined with high volume. Keep your costs as low as possible, reflect those low costs in your pricing and sell a ton.

Design professionals, on the other hand, feel that their status as 'professionals,' their focus on individual projects rather than continuous process, and their strong tradition of 'doing whatever it takes' all conspire against the commodity label. Design professionals pride themselves on the service and quality they offer, rather than high volume and low price.

Unfortunately, quality and service have long since become expected by your clients. If you don't provide those, you aren't even invited to play in the game. In other words, they have become commodities. Take a few minutes and compare your website with those of your main competitors. Does yours really say anything different? Here's some actual copy from an actual engineering firm's website.

> *Acme Engineering is a consulting engineering firm, specializing in the water and wastewater fields. Acme Engineering is an engineering firm that is focused on identifying opportunities and providing solutions for improved reliability and efficiency. Our staff is comprised of engineers and technical experts with water and wastewater experience. We've been there and understand the challenges you go through. We have the experience and resources to support your project needs from conception to start-up.*

And then Acme complains that their clients won't pay premium fees. Why should they!? If you can't clearly explain and demonstrate the added value that you bring, it's impossible for you to justify any fee, let alone one that's higher than your client may be used to or comfortable paying.

If you don't want to attend the Sam Walton School of Business, here's what you must know. First, unless you offer some clear value beyond the basic service, you won't be able to sustain higher prices. Your clients simply won't pay more for a service they perceive to be available elsewhere for less.

Second, you can't offer the frills of a high-end service while charging bargain basement prices. It's simply unsustainable with profit margins that are borderline or worse.

Finally, to maintain your exclusive status, you must continuously change and update that which makes you special. Remember the law of the marketplace: as soon as you offer a unique service that can command a high profit margin, you will attract competitors. As supply increases, prices will automatically be driven down. To remain at the top of the curve, you must regularly introduce new services, features, levels of customer service or other added value. If you don't, you will quickly slide down the well-greased, slippery slope to commodity.

Hourly rates

(Why one hour is never worth another hour)

What is the highest hourly rate your firm has ever charged anybody for doing anything?

I've often asked this question of my seminar attendees and, after 20 years, the highest rate I've encountered is about $350 for very specialized expert witness work. Taken at face value, this means that no one, in any of the thousands of AE firms I've met is capable, in the span of one hour, of doing anything worth more than $350. Does this seem as nutty to you as it does to me?

When was the last time you attended a permitting or zoning meeting on behalf of a client? When was the last time you negotiated a concession in such a meeting? Maybe it was a concession that saved or earned your client tens, or even hundreds of thousands of dollars. What did you bill for that one-hour meeting?

When Frank Lloyd Wright was commissioned to design the house that became Fallingwater, he spent almost nine months without so much as lifting a pencil. One day, unexpectedly, he received a call from the client who announced he was on his way to Wright's studio to see how the design for the house was coming. At that point, Wright sat down and proceeded to draw, in the span of just a few hours, the design that members of the American Institute of Architects voted the "best all-time work of American architecture."

What were those few hours of Wright's time worth? Or, alternatively, should he have been paid for every hour of the nine months during which he continuously turned the project over and over in his mind, reviewing every rock and outcrop of the site? How should a design professional value his or her services?

Too many design professionals believe that they have only their time to sell. They don't manufacture gizmos or broker securities. They think, make recommendations, and work with ideas.

The traditional method of evaluating the cost of these efforts is to measure the length of time expended doing it. This seems logical enough. If I spend 10 hours working on your behalf, and my time is worth $25 per hour, you are happy to compensate me $250.

But design professionals are creative individuals and you can never tell when one is going to spring forth with a brilliant idea. Like most creative endeavors, the idea will appear to come out of nowhere and it could be worth millions. When you are compensated for the value of your ideas we call this value-based pricing.

But when the services you sell are commodities, when identical or very similar services are available from many sources, your clients use a different kind of value pricing — the low price they pay is equal to the low value they place on the services. This also explains why you encounter tremendous resistance to using value-pricing methods for traditional services that are available anywhere.

Many firms hesitate to try value-based pricing for two reasons: First, they are afraid of alienating clients. But the first rule of negotiating is, 'if you don't ask, you won't get.' Second, the inherently risk-averse nature of AEs leads many to shy away from fee arrangements that leave them exposed. Higher profit will always be accompanied by higher risk.

Want to increase the opportunities you firm has for value pricing? Take these steps to look for opportunities.

- Hold an internal discussion to see if your firm is ready for value services and value pricing. The culture and the chutzpah have to be there.
- Learn how other industries and other firms use value pricing. There are several books by Ronald J. Baker that will really open your eyes. Look him up on Amazon. (Ron's mission statement is: "To, once and for all, bury the billable hour and timesheet in the professions")
- Begin with clients with whom you already have a strong relationship. They will be more open to seeing the potential win-win of value pricing.
- Watch for the unique situation. If there is significant value to be added or the circumstances are right, don't hesitate to make the pitch for value pricing.

Value pricing represents a culture change for design professionals. No doubt it will require you to swim upstream, but the effort will pay off handsomely.

Is anyone paying attention?

Let's talk for a minute about audience dynamics in a presentation.

Think back to the last presentation you attended. Maybe it lasted an hour. Did you maintain absolute, unflinching, concentrated focus through the entire presentation? Of course you didn't. Your mind drifts. It wanders off to other thoughts. Maybe things going on at work, things you have to remember to take care of at home, an errand you have to run on your way home that evening. Regardless, your mind wanders all over. The human mind is an enormously difficult thing to control.

As the presentation goes on the level of attention that the audience is paying changes. The good news is that it changes in ways that are highly predictable. At the beginning of any presentation or speech given by anyone the audience is paying a high level of attention. They are thinking, 'this is new, I haven't heard this person speak before, is there something I'm going to learn, what's of value to me?' Early on they are going to be paying close attention.

However, once the speaker is into the presentation, the audience's attention level falls off. Quite steeply, actually. As the presentation rolls on, the audience members are off to many different places — everywhere except here listening to the speaker! Then, as they sense it's coming to an end — "it was a 30 minute presentation, it's been 25 minutes, I guess they'll be wrapping up soon" — they start paying attention because they know they can pick up the gist in the summary. And speakers always oblige by giving a summary.

A good speech writer knows how this dynamic works and they will insert what we call 'attention spikes.' They will write a joke into the speech, which brings everyone back. Or they will tell an interesting anecdote that will bring the audience back to the speaker. But only temporarily, since we know they'll drift off again.

Knowing that the dynamics of audience attention level work this way, how is the typical presentation designed?

When the presenter is first introduced, audience attention levels are very high. But most presenters waste this valuable attention by talking about things that don't matter:

> *'Good morning. I'm really pleased to have this opportunity to present to you today. I'd like to take a moment to tell you a little bit more about our firm and allow you to get to know us personally. Before we get started I'd like to tell you about the history of our company. We've been in business since 1932. Our firm was founded by George Founder and we've grown steadily since. We now have 10 offices in three states...'*

As that boring presenter drones on, imagine that you're watching the dial on an Attention-O-Meter attached to the audience. It's falling fast! They are drifting off. And they're drifting off just as the presenter is about to head into the meat of his presentation. The audience has left the room. They're gone and not listening to all the really important things he has to say. They miss the punch line.

Then, when the audience does return its attention in time for the close, what do we typically do? We wrap up by saying,

> *'I'd like to thank you again for allowing us to be here today and reinforce just how important this project is to us and tell you how committed we are to your satisfaction.'*

The presentation opened with trite statements. Then it closed with trite statements and all the good stuff was put into the part where the audience was missing. It is any wonder that we have so many snoozers during a presentation?

Lincoln didn't begin the Gettysburg address by introducing himself and he didn't close by thanking the audience for their time and attention. A good pitcher will always lead with his best pitch. Let's learn the lesson.

Keeping your audience's attention

(On the edge of their seats instead of asleep in them)

Unless you work to make it otherwise, the audience's attention for your presentation will be high at the beginning and end of your session and low in the middle. Here are some ways to grab their attention early and keep it as much as possible.

You've always known that either first or last in the order of presentations offers an advantage. The firms that present first and last are more likely to stand out and stick in the mind of the client. But the same rule applies within the confines of your own presentation.

Trial lawyers have always known that, in order to persuade a jury, they can rely on two principles: the doctrines of *primacy* and *recency*. Primacy says that you should always lead off with your strongest statement. This catches your audience off guard and leaves a dramatic and indelible first impression. Recency says that you should go out with a bang and leave a lasting impression that stays with the client long after your presentation is over.

From this you might conclude that the very beginning and the very end of your presentation are the best times to communicate your most important information. And you'd be right. This is an opportunity for you to gain some real advantage.

Here are some samples of opening lines and themes you can use in a smack-me-between-the-eyes opening. When I say 'opening line,' that's exactly what I mean. Don't start with, 'good morning,' or 'thank you for inviting us here,' or any other line that your competitor is sure to use. Head straight into the good stuff.

If the client's key hot button is Schedule, you might start with:

> *"This morning we are going to show you how your bridge reconstruction project can actually be completed in less time than you anticipated. We have analyzed the project in depth and we have discovered at least six areas where time*

can be saved. We are going to share these ideas with you today."

If it is Technical Issues:

"As you streamline and automate the city's water filtration and sewage disposal system, you have wisely chosen to integrate their control with the use of a SCADA system. In our meeting today, our chief programmer is going to review the system we intend to design for you to make sure you fully understand how the system will work, what safeguards are built in and how your operators will be trained in the use of the system. We will be illustrating our discussion with case studies from the SCADA systems we have designed and installed for Greenbury and Harpers Mills."

If it is the Approvals Process:

"This project would be a piece of cake if it weren't for the challenge of gaining EPA approval. In our presentation this afternoon, we are going to focus almost exclusively on the process we will use to apply to and then negotiate with the EPA for your VIP (Very Important Permit)."

Construction Costs:

"We are all aware of the instability of construction costs in this market. No one is more concerned about controlling them on your behalf than we at Smith & Jones. In our interview this morning we are going to show you the many techniques we are going to use to ensure that, throughout the design and contract document process, construction costs are estimated and ensured as closely as possible."

Compare any of these bold openings with the boring old, *"We are pleased to be presenting to you today..."* Any client, with those hot buttons front and center in their mind, will sit up and pay attention.

Raising the Attention-O-Meter

If you remember our imaginary Attention-O-Meter, the attention level of your audience drops dramatically during the middle of your interview. By injecting an item of interest, a story or introducing a physical prop, you can reclaim the attention you're losing. Attention spikes are simply verbal or visual devices that bring a group back together. For example:

"In summary..."
Don't wait until the end of the show. You can summarize as often as you like. Each time, you will get everyone's attention back because they don't want to miss the important point.

"Now I'm going to show you..."
Words like this indicate that something new is about to happen. They want to see if it has relevance for them so they will tune back in while you introduce the new topic.

"I know you'll appreciate this..."
This speaks directly to your client's search for direct benefits. If you say they will appreciate something, they don't want to miss out.

"Here's something you may not have known..."
This appeals to the natural curiosity that is embedded in human nature. Everyone is bound to sit up and pay attention when you open a paragraph with this phrase.

"Let's take a look at..."
This brings you and the audience together in a joint activity. You are also giving the audience an instruction that they are happy to follow.

In any presentation, your first obligation is to address the client's question: "What's in it for me?" If you can't do that at the very beginning, you won't have their interest in the first place and you won't be able to regain what you never had.

Why aren't you paid more?

If we want to escape the commodities trap, the burden is on us to communicate and then deliver extraordinarily high value that is unlike anything the competition can dish up.

I've been reading some excellent marketing books lately and came across a related passage in one that I simply have to share:

> *Value: The difference between the anticipated price and the marked price. If the marked price is lower than the anticipated price, the value is perceived as good. If the marked price is higher than the anticipated price, the value is perceived as poor. (There is no profit in lowering the marked price; you must raise the anticipated price.)*

> Roy H. Williams, *Secret Formulas of the Wizard of Ads*

This industry whines endlessly about poor fees, the constant undercutting of prices and the lack of appreciation that clients have for the value of what you do. But we need to turn this discussion around and take responsibility.

The first thing that we need to realize is that any client who perceives that there is a value to be had from you that isn't obtainable elsewhere, will be happy to pay the higher price. This is proven day after day as stores, restaurants, businesses and yes, even design professionals across the country, charge significantly higher prices than do available alternates.

If price were the only thing, then everyone driving around out there in a Mercedes Benz would be clinically insane. Why would they pay $120,000 for four wheels and an engine, when for one fifth of that, they can have a perfectly reliable Chevy? Why would anyone eat at Chez Pierre when McDonald's has a Big Mac, Coke and fries for less than five bucks? Why? Because they perceive the difference in value for their money.

But first they have to perceive the difference and the higher value. Take 15 minutes and do a quick survey of your competitor's websites. Besides a different list of projects, do you see anything that is truly unique? Do you see anything that stands out from the crowd? Of course not! All our marketing looks and sounds the same. It's boring, unimaginative and predictable. Would <u>you</u> pay a premium price for that?

Your clients need the services you sell. But when they know they can find the same thing down the street for less, they're going to go there. Your job is to communicate and then follow through on a promise that your clients get something different from you. Something worth more.

When was the last time you introduced a new service? When was the last time you adjusted the services you offer to keep in tune with, or ahead of the needs of, your clients? When was the last time you stopped offering an old service because the profit margins had slipped and you were happy to let the others fight over the meager fees? When did you last think about the various components of the services you offer and the potential for separating, repackaging, or combining them with non-traditional services to increase the perceived and actual value?

When was the last time you wondered if a different marketing approach could tell a story about the real value you offer? Not the same ol' some ol', but something different, something that really stood up and got attention. When will be the last time you complain about being underpaid?

And that means...

You know the difference between features and benefits. A feature of the car is that it has 27 airbags. The benefit to the car buyer is that she is much more likely to emerge unharmed after an accident. Bottom line: clients don't buy the features of your firm, they buy benefits that will make their lives easier, less complicated and more successful.

In a recent book I was reading I came across an amazing technique to help keep your marketing efforts focused on client benefits rather than features of your firm. It works like this: Silently add the words, 'which means...' to the end of every statement you make in your proposals and sales presentations. This will remind you to always translate the features of your firm into benefits for the client.

Let's look at some typical examples:

"Our firm was founded in 1958."
...which means that more than half a century of accumulated 'lessons-learned' will eliminate potential mistakes and bring many time- and money-saving ideas to your project.

"Our company has an excellent on-site safety record."
...which means you enjoy lower insurance and overall project costs, peace of mind and happy workers while avoiding negative public relations.

"Our firm has won numerous industry awards."
...which means you share the prestige and recognition and take comfort in our extremely high standard of excellence.

"We have an excellent track record of successful projects."
...which means you will have fewer demands on your time, better decision-making, reduced risk and a much higher likelihood of on-time and on-budget delivery.

"Our firm is the largest in the state."

…which means you enjoy reduced costs through buying power and increased speed through our leverage of suppliers and subcontractors.

"We have the greatest people in the world working here."

…which means that you will enjoy pampered attention, ease of communication, an extended network and easy, timely access to important information.

"Our firm has invested heavily in reliable systems and procedures."

…which means you can trust the information we provide while enjoying reduced risk and the ability to focus your attention on other priorities.

"Our management team is heavily involved in the community."

…which means you benefit from an extended network, the prestige of working with a community leader and direct links to additional opportunities.

I believe you get the point. Your customers and prospects don't care about the features of your company. They only care about the benefits that will accrue to them. So follow your statements with, 'which means…' in order to focus on the benefits and leave the discussion of features to your came-in-second competitor.

Left brain, right brain — Let's go marketing

Every time I land safely in an airplane and every time I make it to the far side of a bridge I say a silent one in thanks for all the wonderful engineers in the world and their fabulous, left-brained thinking. I have enormous admiration and appreciation for the logic, the rationale, and the discipline required to be an engineer.

But when it comes to persuading a client to buy your services, a larger dose of right brain would go a long way.

Engineers think, and have been trained to communicate in ways that are logical, factual and rational. A well-written technical paper, for example, lets the reader evaluate the facts and not be influenced by hype, opinion or emotion. But when these communication techniques are used in proposals and marketing materials you risk boring and even alienating all the non-technical, non-engineer types who might be making important decisions about hiring you. Not everybody thinks like an engineer. In fact, the population has a broad spectrum of communication preferences.

Cognitive Psychology is an entire science devoted to studying how people take in information, process it, and reach decisions. And the non-technical people of the world communicate and understand best, not through the sorting of facts and data, but through stories, allegory, examples and —yes — emotion.

It's a bit of an over-simplification, but it's quite safe to say that communication preferences are linked to the four basic personality types:

- The person who values intellect needs to understand your logic.
- The person who values feelings needs to perceive your motives.
- The person who values stability needs to know it has been tested.
- The person who values courage needs to hear you speak of action.

The best writers, speakers, and presenters speak to each of these four people every time they attempt to persuade. Putting something into your proposal or presentation for each of them broadens your conversation and makes it easier for each individual to positively connect with you.

Most of us attempt to persuade as though everyone makes decisions according to the same criteria we use. Read the lyrics of a Bob Dylan song and it's pretty apparent that this guy ain't an engineer! Now read an excerpt from any recent proposal from your firm. Is it any wonder you're not entering many poetry contests?

People don't all communicate in the same way. Learn to speak to all four preferences and your voice will carry rich, persuasive harmony.

Light a fire in your presentation

I devour books voraciously and I recently came across a gem: *Public Speaking As Listeners Like It!,* by Richard C. Borden. It's old, long out of print, and, based on the sensibilities of 1935 vs. today, as politically incorrect as you can get. (e.g., It would appear that, in 1935, only men gave or listened to speeches!)

But once through all the quaint period issues, the book makes some fabulous points, as pertinent to your presentation today as they were 80 years ago. I particularly like 'ol Richard's advice on opening a speech or presentation:

> *In the first section of your speech — start a fire! Your speech is not well organized unless you kindle a quick flame of spontaneous interest in your first sentence.*
> *When you rise to make a speech, do not picture your audience as waiting with eager eyes and bated breath to catch your message.*
> *Picture it, instead, as definitely bored — and distinctly suspicious that you are going to make this situation worse. Picture your listeners as looking uneasily at their watches, stifling yawns and giving vent to a unanimous 'HO HUM!' The first sentence of your speech must crash through your audience's initial apathy. Don't open your speech on Safety by saying: 'The subject which has been assigned me is the reduction of traffic accidents.' Say, instead: 'Four hundred and fifty shiny new coffins were delivered to this city last Thursday.'*

Mr. Borden is absolutely right. Your audience, or the selection panel for your interview is not sitting on the edges of their seats, waiting to hear your every word. They are anticipating another boring, monotonous speaker with an endless supply of PowerPoint bullets. When you open with, *"Good morning. We're really pleased to have this opportunity to present to you today...'* they know that there is a pleasant snooze in their immediate future.

Predictable, boring, and commonplace are not the ingredients of a 'Holy Cow!' presentation. Think of the opening sequence of any James Bond film. It puts you on the edge of your seat from the first frame and keeps you there through the entire movie. Snoozing is not an option!

Yes, it might feel a little uncomfortable to open with a statement that is controversial, provocative and totally unexpected. But it will light a fire under the seats of your audience and have them hanging on every word that follows.

Why it's so easy to sell Volvos

It used to be that 'branding' was for soap, soft drinks and cars. No longer. Your brand is as important to the growth and prosperity of your firm as it is to Coke, Tide and BMW.

A brand isn't a logo, a tag line or the latest advertising scheme dreamed up by the Mad Men. Instead, a brand is the sum total of all the mental associations, good and bad, that are triggered by a company name.

Taken a step further, a brand is a promise. A promise of quality, consistency and reliability that's known and trusted far beyond your firm's client list. That promise isn't made through marketing or advertising. That would be too easy. Instead, it's made by consistent performance over time. But here's the twist: In order to grow, that great performance must be aggressively broadcast through marketing communications, promotions and advertising as well as enthusiastically spread by word-of-mouth.

Then, because the dependability of your promise is so well known, new customers feel safe in using your brand even without personal experience. At the same time, existing and past customers are confident they'll receive the same quality and reliability when coming back to work with you again.

There are two sides to a branding effort:

1.   *Making the promise with marketing*
Traditional marketing for design professionals focuses heavily on business development and sales, with the bulk of our time spent chasing individual projects. The effort is highly dependent on specific individuals and the quality of their relationships.

Brand-based marketing balances that sales effort with an equal emphasis on promotion. A strong promotional effort can build name recognition and enhance your reputation with regular repetition of a positive message over a significantly larger base.

2.   *Delivering the promise through execution*
Any business that builds a strong brand image is driven by *process*. It establishes a successful process for accomplishing its work, then manages that process. Individual projects come and

go, but the process by which they are developed and completed gives the company its strength and competitive advantage. Customers depend on this consistent, reliable process to deliver the same unfailing service time after time.

Too often design professionals are *project* driven. They work from one project to the next with less regard for a standardized process that would make the production of work faster, easier, more accurate and more reliable. In short, they work with little regard for building a brand image.

Volvo has been successfully selling cars in North America since 1955 because it adopted this two-pronged branding strategy. First, every Volvo ad that you've ever seen has included the word 'Safety' and demonstrated how safety was an integral part of their cars. Second, Volvo has consistently led the industry with safety innovations that, in many cases, have been introduced years before other manufacturers. In other words, Volvo followed through on the advertising promise.

As a part of its strong brand Volvo has come to 'own' the word 'safety' in the automotive business. The net result? No one mistakenly walks onto a Volvo dealer's lot. They go there on purpose to buy a Volvo. So how hard is it to sell Volvos?

There is a huge lesson in this for you:

Is there a word or phrase that everyone immediately thinks of when your firm name is mentioned? How frequently, regularly and relentlessly have you communicated the essence of your brand to your entire target market? Not just current and past clients, but everyone. Volvo's target market is affluent urban dwellers between 25 and 54. Do you suppose there is anyone in the US, fitting that description, who has NOT heard the Volvo message? And finally, how consistent is your project delivery with the promises you're making in your marketing?

I was speaking with an engineer about the branding efforts his firm should be undertaking. He was reluctantly convinced that it was important but then asked, "How long do I have to keep this up?"

My answer: When Coke, Ford and McDonald's (and Volvo) decide that they've done enough, you can stop too.

Your Brand is NOT…

The concept of brand is still somewhat new in the design professions and there is a lot of misunderstanding. For example, I've often heard firms saying they are going to 're-brand' themselves, when in fact they're simply coming up with a new logo. Let's talk about some things that your brand is NOT.

Your Logo
Your logo (if you even have one — and there is no requirement that you do) is a visual image, intended to represent the company. Like your company name, it's the thing that is (ideally) remembered with 'positive predisposition.' That's marketing-speak for, 'they like you.' But the mental associations, good and bad, that are triggered by a logo are the same ones your customers and the marketplace have learned to connect with your company name.

The real value of a logo is the instant visual association that can be garnered with just a glance. No need to read anything. No need to take time to make sure you understand. Just a quick flash of that 'swoosh' and we all know it's Nike.

Despite all the angst that goes into developing a logo, it really doesn't matter what it looks like or what color it is, so long as you treat it consistently. Green, pink, round or square — just make sure that your target market sees the same thing over and over and over again.

Your Tagline
The same angst that is invested in logo development is also put into the creation of a company tagline. But regardless of what you write, your customers will develop their own taglines based on their assessment of your quality and performance.

A famous instance of a customer-developed tagline involved the Italian carmaker FIAT. During a period when their products were notoriously unreliable, drivers determined that FIAT stood for Fix It Again, Tony. Not what the corporate marketers had in mind!

By all means develop and use a tagline. But make sure your project quality, attention to detail, and customer service are consistent with it or your clients will develop one of their own to reflect your REAL brand.

What you say it is

As with the FIAT drivers, your brand is determined by the marketplace, not your marketing department. It is your customers who will decide what your company is best known for.

That doesn't mean you have no control. You must set out to establish your brand. But without consistent harmony between what you promise in your marketing and what you deliver in your projects, you will never control your brand.

You can launch the most aggressive brand-building campaign ever. But that brand will always be tested and confirmed by your clients. They are the ones who get to say what your brand is all about.

Permanent

Your firm is not what it was 10 years ago. And it's not what it will be 10 years from now. As the firm evolves so does the brand and you need to be aware of and proactive about its evolution.

Volkswagen is a very different brand today than it was when the first Beetle was introduced to the North American market in the 1960s. Likewise with Honda and Toyota. But these companies have slowly and carefully guided the transformation of their brands from cheap economy car to world-class automobile. The marketing promises have not outstripped the product quality and we consumers have been happy to let those companies guide our understanding of their brands.

It takes hard work to build and maintain a strong brand. It's assailed all the time from many sides with competitors taking pot shots, disgruntled customers or former employees raking muck and the odd black eye when delivering a project.

But it's worth all that effort. Well-known companies such as Coke and Nordstrom's count the equity of their brand as a huge plus on the balance sheet. You can get that kind of equity and value from a strong brand image too. Today would be a good day to start!

Practical market research

So you're about to respond to an RFP. Before you zip off one of your standard proposals, I invite you to think about something. Do your proposals really zero-in on the particular needs and circumstances of each client, or are they generic documents that look and read much the same no matter who they go to?

To laser target your proposals and dramatically increase your hit rate, a little detective work is in order. Your objective will be to collect as much information about the client, the project, the selection process, the competition, and the surrounding circumstances as possible. The more you know about your customer and their project, the better chance your proposal has.

Step one is to set a deadline! The business schools teach you how to conduct extensive and thorough market research. But you don't have time for that. The good news is that 95% of what you need to know is probably already in your head. You just have to shake it out!

So give yourself a time limit. There's almost no end to the information you can dig up, but at some point you must take the material you've collected, and move forward with the proposal. Depending on the size and importance of the project, your time limit might be two weeks, two days or two hours. It doesn't matter. Set the limit, dig as fast and as deep as you can, then stop and work with the material you have collected.

What should you look to discover?

Regarding the client

What is their business and how does it operate? Who are the key decision-makers? How large is this company or agency? Are they growing, holding steady, or shrinking? Is there a strong 'personality' to the organization? What is its history? What are its main strengths and weaknesses? Have they designed or built other projects before? What are their expectations? Do they emphasize service and quality or price?

Regarding the project

What is the history of its development? What is it expected to accomplish for the owners and the end users? Can you visit an existing facility and speak with the users? How will the project be funded? Are there any significant political issues or special interest groups involved with the project? What are the challenges on the project?

Regarding the selection process

How is the selection to be made? What are the stated selection criteria? What is the relative weighting of each selection point? Who is on and who is in charge of the selection committee? Is there any political wrangling on the committee? What are the expectations regarding size, sophistication and content of a proposal and interview? Are there specific minority set-aside requirements for the project?

That's a big list of information to collect and it's unlikely you'll ever be able to check off every item. But the Internet and the telephone are wonderful inventions, holding more useful information than you might ever imagine! Every bit of information you can discover will give you an edge in understanding, focus and likelihood of winning.

The five obligations of a marketing department

OK, this one might sting a little.

I believe that it's long past time for AE marketers to significantly raise their game. It's also way past time that Owners and Principals stand back and let their marketing team do the jobs they've been trained and hired for. Serious, sophisticated marketing strategies are required for a firm to grow and thrive today and most firms are falling far short of that mark.

Why? I see two problem areas. First, firm owners and principals somehow feel that they know more about marketing than the experts they've hired to do it for them. Just because you have a degree, a license and decades of experience as an engineer does not mean you are an expert in how to sell those services. We're well into the 21st century and the bar of sophistication has gone way, way up. Your ability to judge what's good and what works has not kept up.

Second, marketers are failing to show leadership and creativity in the role they play in their firms. Yes, I've heard all about how the boss won't let you. But it's your job to educate the boss and find a way. And that's simply not happening.

Today and beyond I believe that the marketing staff in every AE firm — whether that consists of a single individual or an entire team — has a set of responsibilities. I call it the five obligations of a Marketing Department

1.   To Learn

They must remain lifelong students of marketing. Learn how marketing really works, not just in the AE industry but in all industries. Because the techniques we're using to sell AE services today were invented more than 100 years ago by the people who are still selling soap, cars and timeshare condos. And we need to catch up. We need to know what they know — the principles behind marketing, the psychology of persuasion. Study the masters — David Ogilvie, Al Ries, Jack Trout, Seth Godin, Jay Conrad Levinson. The list goes on. You can't sell something if you don't know how selling works.

2. *To Stretch*

Marketers must always be stretching, testing and experimenting with their ideas. When was the last time your firm tried something new and really different? Have you looked outside our industry to see what they're doing to sell other goods and services? Can you really call your marketing strategy 'creative?' Is it really any different from what the other guy is doing? When was the last time you tried something so different that you failed spectacularly and learned some really great lessons? What might your Super Bowl ad look like?

3. *To Question*

There is a lot of conventional wisdom surrounding AE marketing efforts. But is all of it right? Even if it did apply at one time, does it still apply? Is it really true that it's all about relationships? If so, how did the low-cost firm steal your long-term client? Is PowerPoint the answer to every presentation? Is CRM going to solve your cross-selling challenges? What if a lot of conventional wisdom was actually kinda stupid?

4. *To Guide*

When I was the VP of Sales and Marketing at a big construction company I made sure that every single day I would get out of my office and visit all the business unit leaders in the company. Sometimes I'd just stick my head in the door, sometimes it would be 15 minutes, sometimes we'd go to lunch. But every time I would use the opportunity to teach them something about marketing. "Here's what my marketing team is working on for you." "Here's what we're going to do for your business unit." "Here's the marketing principle that's behind it." After six months I had some really great partners who had a much better understanding of how marketing works.

5. *To Inspire*

This is a tough, competitive and high-stress business and it's easy to get down and cry the blues over just about everything. Somebody needs to maintain the sunny outlook and that should be the job of marketing. If anybody in the company ought to be capable of and responsible for high spirits, it's those who have been trained to be inherently optimistic and creative. We need a steady supply of optimism, enthusiasm and energy. I look to the Marketing Department for that infusion.

We spend so much time wringing our hands about how to differentiate one firm from the next. But the easiest and most powerful differentiator in the world would be a creative, energetic and sophisticated marketing strategy that put your company in front of a huge number of prospective clients over and over and over again. Who's going to have the nerve to be different?

The most important thing to leave behind after a presentation

I'm frequently asked two questions:

- *What should I leave behind with the audience or review panel following my presentation?*
- *Can I get a copy of your presentation?*

The answer to the second question is invariably 'No.' And the primary reason is that my slides, without me there to present around them, are meaningless. If my slides were self-sufficient and could be read and understood on their own, why did we gather for a presentation? Why didn't I just send a memo?

The answer to the first question is a little more complex. Of course you know enough to not hand out copies of your presentation to the audience before you begin. They'll read through it and then be off in their own world, paying no attention to you because they already know everything you're going to talk about.

But a leave-behind can increase memorability following your presentation and a souvenir will have them remembering you for days or weeks.

I am a staunch opponent of the PowerPoint presentation that's filled with bullet points that we all read together. It puts an audience to sleep, it's boring and, as a result, fails to engage and excite. For all these reasons I never recommend leaving behind a print-out of your slide deck.

But there are some things that you might choose to leave behind:

- A white paper or article on the same topic as the presentation
- Supplementary information providing additional detail or back-up data

- A printed page with names, contact information and photos of the presenter(s).
- Specifications and information about the product or service you've just spoken about
- Bags of jelly beans

There is, however, one thing that you must ALWAYS leave behind following your presentation. If you gave the presentation in order to persuade, inform, excite and engage your audience. If you were enthusiastic and authentic. If energy and optimism flowed out from you. If you sparked interest and dialogue then you have already left behind the most important thing:

A powerful and lasting impression.

Lessons from Walt Disney

It takes a lot of effort to keep yourself out of the commodity game. Five minutes after you start your exciting new business, three competitors open across the street, all of whom seem happy to steal your ideas and undercut your pricing. While this sounds depressingly like Sisyphus, doomed forever to push the rock up the hill, only to have it roll back, this is also the excitement, the challenge, and the creativity of entrepreneurship.

Back in the 1920s a young illustrator penned a charming character that became known as Mickey Mouse. By combining the character with the emerging technologies of animation and sound, Walt Disney was the first to produce a cartoon with synchronized sound. *Steamboat Willie* was released in 1928 and was an immediate hit. Disney made good money. Then the competitors showed up.

Walt's strong entrepreneurial spirit wouldn't allow him to be one of many, so in 1937 he made a really long cartoon, colored in the pictures and audiences flocked to see Snow White and her seven dwarfs, the first full-length, full-color, animated feature film. And more competitors came.

By the mid-1950s animated cartoons and movies had become commonplace, and Disney wanted more. This time he took his characters, combined them with 160 acres outside Los Angeles, and created Disneyland. While the world had plenty of cartoon characters and amusement parks, no one had ever seen a theme park before, and the profits rolled in.

Then, in 1970, with theme parks popping up around the country, Disney again stayed ahead of the pack by turning a day at the park in Anaheim into a family vacation in Orlando.

Since then Disney has continued to expand by exploring new ideas. Today it is feature film studios, cruise lines, real estate development, and all manner of profitable ventures. This type of continuous reinvention and business creativity has kept Disney fresh, alive, and at the forefront of business success for the better part of a century.

Interestingly, Disney's business creativity not only includes new business ventures, it is equally driven by *letting go of old ideas that are no longer viable.* The last new Mickey Mouse cartoon was created in 1953!

Every time the competition tries to catch up, Disney brings out its creative muscle to reinvent and repackage the products and services it offers, introduce new ideas, and prune out dead wood.

When was the last time you introduced a new service? When was the last time you adjusted the services you offer to keep in tune with, or ahead of the needs of, your clients? When was the last time you stopped offering an old service because the profit margins had slipped and competition was too intense?

When was the last time you thought carefully about the value you bring to your customers, rather than the total number of hours you've worked multiplied by your billing rate?

Do logos, colors and company names matter?

One of my (many) heroes is an advertising genius by the name of Roy H. Williams. He quite deservedly goes by the nickname — The Wizard of Ads. In one of his weekly emails Roy talks about the power (or lack thereof) of logos, colors and company names. Since I have a number of clients who are currently embroiled in the agonizing task of revisiting logos, names and colors I thought I'd share Roy's thoughts.

Roy asks this question:

> *Could a company win if its logo was indistinctive and boring and literally gray?*

And I'm going to let Roy speak from here.

> *A schmuck falls off the balcony on the 30th floor. A putz is the guy he lands on.*
> *A putz is passively stupid; ridiculously unlucky.*
> *Could a company succeed with a name like Putzmeister?*
> *Putzmeister is a real company that was founded by Karl Schlecht in 1958. Today it employs 3,900 people that produce more than $ 1.5 billion in annual sales in 154 countries on 5 continents, name and logo and color be damned. By the way, that's billion with a 'B.'*
> *Wal-Mart may have the dumbest name in the history of the world. "My name is Walton, so I'll call the store Wal-Mart." Really? And yet he became so rich that just six of his descendants are worth more today than the combined net worth of 30 percent of our nation. That's right, a tiny company begun in 1962 with an idiotic name and a drab logo and an unimaginative color scheme became the most successful retail empire in the history of the world in less than 30 years.*
> *And they never bothered to change the name or the logo.*
> *I meet Chicken Little advertising people every day who squeal, "the sky is falling" over names and colors and*

logos.

Color is a language. It definitely matters. A little.

Shape is a language. It can contradict or reinforce your choice of colors. Shape matters. A little.

Product and company names are words that carry conscious and unconscious associations. They absolutely matter. But what matters most of all is what matters to the customer.

Customers who buy from your competitors aren't choosing your competitors because they have better logos. Your problem is something else entirely.

Customers care about things like products and procedures and policies that might affect them. They care about your offers and assurances. They care about the experience you create for them.

Will your client be glad they chose you? Yes? How are communicating this? What do you offer as evidence? Testimonials are suspect. Bold promises sound like Ad-speak. What are you doing to give your prospective client real confidence that choosing you is the right thing to do?

And be sure to check out Roy's website at www.rhw.com

We can all improve our game

The majority of firms derive between 70% and 90% of their total volume from repeat work. What a wonderful story that tells about how well you're treating those clients, how loyal they are to you and what a great relationship you enjoy!

But what about that 10 to 30 percent who DON'T come back? Here are a few random thoughts about keeping those clients and finding new ones to replace those that leave.

Nurture your network

The work you get comes from people you know and the more people you know, the more work you'll get. It's too easy to spend time in the office, head down, buried in technical work or pushing administrative paper. But no one hires you for the time you spend in your office. They hire you because they know you, trust you and believe you'll look after them.

Your network of friends and business associates is your lifeline. It feeds you work, it connects you to opportunity and it supports you when you're hurting. But a network doesn't come looking for you. You have to seek it out, develop it, nurture it and make it grow. How many new friends and business connections have you made in the past 60 days? (btw — simply sending a LinkedIn request doesn't count!)

Cast a wider net

Who's on your mailing list and how often do you contact them? Most mailing lists contain only those people we've worked with — current and past clients, consultants and contractors and maybe a few friends. And we send them something at holiday time. The best lists, on the other hand, the ones that really produce results, don't limit themselves to the people we know, they include the people we'd LIKE to know. Those future clients you haven't yet worked with, but with whom you'd love to work.

Here's a great tip: add your competitors' clients to your mailing list. How do you know they aren't dissatisfied and ready to look around?

Win work away from a complacent competitor

In tough times your clients (and your competitor's clients) question everything. They want to know if they're really getting their money's worth. This is a great time to get your foot in the door with a new client that has been handing their work to a competitor. Base your pitch on the premise that they owe it to themselves to ensure they're getting the best value. Ask for a small project and encourage them to compare. If they see that you have better customer service, better quality and competitive pricing, they may be tempted to shift their allegiance to you.

Raise the bar on customer service

Every one of your competitors can produce the same great quality of technical work that you can. (That's why we call them 'competitors!') So why should a client choose to hire you instead of the other guy? Over-the-top customer service will give you a competitive edge that technical expertise and even low price can never overcome. You've experienced great customer service (just not often enough) and you know that you're willing to pay extra for it.

Imagine that you operate a store. But instead of clothing or groceries, your store sells engineering or architecture. What's it like to shop at your store? What do customers experience when they come in? How are they greeted? Are they made to feel wanted and welcome? How are they treated by the staff? What are they thinking when they leave? What can you do to improve that experience and make it more pleasant and memorable?

Thinking outside the awards box

Recently I attended an awards dinner. Three and a half hours of talented people being recognized by their peers for their high quality work. The free meal and the Chardonnay were pretty good too! But it got me thinking...

There's a long and venerable tradition among design firms of participating in programs that bestow awards for excellence. Winning an award can enhance the quality of work your firm produces, build morale and (hopefully) enhance your prestige.

But depending on the circumstances of the award and how you follow up, it may or may not have any marketing value.

There are two categories of awards: those given by your peers — including professional associations and journals — and those sponsored by clients.

Let's say you enter and win an AIA, ACEC or ASCE award. While it's great that you won and probably generated some pride and warm fuzzy feelings around the office, the only ones who will know that you won will be your peers and competitors. And they're just annoyed that they didn't win!

Peer-based awards are great to enter and win, but their marketing value is entirely up to you. When you win (or are even nominated) issue an immediate press release and make the award the subject of your next direct mail piece. Put a big announcement on your website, then tweet and blog about it. And don't simply report that you won the award. Let your audience know that in the process of winning you've developed new capabilities, learned important lessons and acquired new skills.

In contrast, when you win an award sponsored by your client's trade association, that group will do your marketing for you! They'll issue the press release and do your bragging for you! In fact, think of all the potential clients sitting at the rubber chicken dinner, watching as you get recognized as the best in the business. Why not let someone else enhance your reputation for you?

There's a third type of awards program that almost no one takes advantage of: Why don't YOU be the one to sponsor the competition and give the award?

Let's say your firm is involved in the healthcare industry. You sponsor a program in which the children in the pediatric wards of all the local hospitals are invited to 'design' their ideal hospital room. You supply the kits that include crayons, construction paper, scissors, tape and glue to be distributed to all the children in the wards. Then you enlist local celebrities and politicians to judge the competition. It won't be difficult at all to get lots of attention and press coverage because your 'judges' crave the attention too and will put their own media machines to work on your behalf.

Prizes can be as simple as a government savings bond for each of the winners. If you're involved in the K-12 education market you could make something similar work for the school kids.

The point is for you to get creative and see how your firm could begin to recognize and reward excellence on the other side of the table. By reversing the award sponsorship, you control the publicity and reap the marketing and public relations benefits.

A fitness test for your mailing list

Without even looking I can tell that your contact list is out of shape. It's too small, too scrawny and too weak. Time to whip it into shape!

A good mailing/emailing list is the foundation of your brand-building efforts. Though many firms have a mailing list of sorts, they are generally poorly organized, incomplete and difficult to work with. To be an effective tool in your promotional efforts a good mail list has to be robust and flexible.

A comprehensive list will eventually include:

- Every client you are currently working for
- Every client you have ever worked for in the past
- Every client you'd like to work for in the future
- Every client who is currently or has ever worked with your competitors
- Every key decision maker within those client organizations
- Every person in a key decision-making or decision-influencing role in your target markets

This will be far more names than most firms have on their lists. But you need this long list because every one of those companies will eventually need what you sell. Every one represents potential work for you. And every one of those people is in a position to select or influence the selection of your firm.

It's going to take some serious Googling and investigation in directories, industry associations, Chambers of Commerce, etc. And it's going to take time. But since marketing is, in some respects, a 'numbers game,' you can't afford to ignore anyone on your list as a potential client.

A good start to your mailing list will have 50 to 100 names for every employee in the firm.

In addition to names, your list will also include other information about these prospects. At the very least you need to record:

- The person's title or position within the company
- Company name

- Address
- Phone
- Email
- Status (are they a current client, past client, prospect, etc.)
- Target market category
- The type of organization (manufacturing, government agency, school district, etc.)

Optionally, you could also maintain fields that describe:

- Names of projects that you've completed for them
- Revenue you have received from them
- Mailings you have sent to them
- Sales contacts you have made with them

All this information can only be maintained in a database. Don't try to keep your mailing list in a word processing program — it simply doesn't have the flexibility to search, sort and output information in the variety of formats you'll need such as mail merges, labels and analysis. I've talked about CRM systems before and they're a great solution. Just make sure you use it for the capability it provides.

Don't confuse a comprehensive contact list with your 'Christmas Card list.' That list, which is still important, likely includes your current clients, sub-consultants, vendors, and maybe even a few friends and casual acquaintances. You can easily combine your card list with your database by adding a radio button titled 'Holiday Card.' A simple search will then produce your mail labels at holiday time.

Once your list is established, it must be maintained. Keep all the mail and email that's returned because the address is incorrect, the person is not longer with the company or the company is no longer in business. Have all the principals and project managers collect names and business cards of individuals who should be on the list. Every three months have someone sit down and enter all the corrections.

The development and maintenance of a contact list like this will take time, effort and commitment — it could easily take six months to initially set up. But it does not require high-cost executive involvement. It is the sort of project that can be handled by a clerical assistant or even a student intern. But the benefits to your brand-building and marketing efforts will be well worth the effort.

Direct Mail — It Ain't Always Junk

I can hear the complaints now — what's the difference between direct mail and junk mail? And don't we all have enough unwelcome junk landing in our mailboxes every day? While you may have had your fill of credit card pre-approvals and scratch-and-sniff perfume promotions, keep two things in mind:

1. You get so much direct mail because the strategy works. If it weren't so successful, the flow would have stopped long ago.

2. Your efforts don't have to resemble the Publisher's Clearinghouse. Yours can be a very classy campaign that reflects the professionalism of your firm.

A successful program uses a mailing list built on criteria that precisely describe your best potential customers. (See the last article for details) You then develop a series of messages that addresses the specific needs and interests of that group and show how the services you offer fulfill those needs. Careful list management means that only those qualified to buy or influence the buying of your services are getting your message and the message they're getting puts you in a very positive light.

What should you send? The best direct mail programs are labeled 'content marketing' — in which you send the prospect tips, advice or other information that they can actively use in their business or agency. While announcements of project wins and new hires can be integrated into a program, by themselves they are of little interest to the people on your list. Instead, keep them up to date with regulatory changes, cost information, market trends, emerging technologies and cost-saving ideas.

Regardless of the material you send, the keys to success in direct mail are frequency and regularity. One-time mailings are just a waste of paper and postage. If you plan to mail your new brochure to your complete mailing list and it's the only thing they'll receive from you all year, don't bother. On the day it arrives a high percentage of the intended recipients will either be out of the office, too busy to read it, or so absorbed with other priorities that your message will be completely lost.

However, sending your message on a regular basis assures that every one of those prospects will not only learn who you are and the value of your services, they'll gradually come to regard you as a significant player in the market. Although what you send is important, it's less important than the fact that your message is received frequently and regularly.

What is an appropriate frequency and regularity? Most importantly, it's one that you can maintain. There is no point in embarking on a direct mail program if you don't have the resources and commitment to maintain regular mailings. Second, it's one that will cross your clients' desk often enough to get their attention, but not so frequently as to annoy them. Generally this means mailings that are no closer than one month apart and no more spread out than quarterly.

Don't expect to be overwhelmed by a flood of responses. The goal of direct mail is NOT to win projects, it's to build name recognition and enhance your reputation. Of all the people you're contacting, very few will need to be speaking with you at any given point. Even if no one responds to any given mailing, rest assured that everyone is becoming familiar with your firm and will call you when the time is right.

The storekeeper

Every one of us has had the experience of walking into a store with the intention of buying a new shirt, blouse, pair of shoes… whatever. And then, not three minutes later, walking back out of the store having decided that not only are we never going to shop there again, we're going to make it a personal mission that no one else ever does either.

And we've also had the opposite experience — walking into the store expecting to buy a shirt, and coming out two hours later with an entire wardrobe.

Both those decisions had nothing to do with price or product availability. They were both driven by the way you were treated by the store clerks. In the first instance they were too busy chatting to realize you were there and their body language shouted that they weren't interested in serving you. In the second store, you were made to feel like you were the most important person on earth, nothing was too much trouble and the clerk had all the time in the world for you.

So, what's it like to shop at your AE store?

Your customers walk in and order 'Ten pounds of engineering please!' What is that experience like? How are they greeted and treated while they're in your store? What is it like to phone into your office? You've had the experience of phoning a company and then being made to feel like you were a disturbance rather than a customer. And you've also had the opposite experience — being made to feel like they'd been waiting for your call. All these little things add up to a big impression that makes a customer want to stay or to look elsewhere.

A large store chain may spend millions on advertising. (You spend thousands on your marketing programs.) The store carefully ensures that the shelves are stocked with the right inventory. (You make sure your staff is trained and equipped to effectively do your work.) They continually rework the look of the store so it appeals to potential customers. (You massage your proposals to make them more appealing.) They do relentless market surveys to ensure their pricing is in line with their competition. All this work will be successful in bringing a new customer in the door.

Then it's up to the store clerk.

In many ways, our project managers and project delivery teams are like those store clerks. Your firm may work tirelessly to attract new clients. You may spend thousands chasing and winning a particular project. But it is only when the client has the chance to experience the service available from the project delivery team, will they decide whether or not to 'shop at your store' again.

Personal business development plans

Everyone should be involved in business development!

That's a refrain that's been echoing around this business forever. Ever seen it happen? Didn't think so. Me neither.

The reason it never happens is two-fold: First, except for that vague platitude, there's very little instruction provided. No one ever tells 'everyone' exactly how they're supposed to be involved in business development, what their contribution ought to be and how they should balance it with their chargeable responsibilities.

Second, the general understanding is that business development consists of a lot of socializing, handshaking, small talk, lunches, general client schmoozing and, horror of horrors, selling! I've never taken a scientific poll, but my informal research indicates that the vast majority of 'everyone' in this business would rather smack themselves with a hammer than get out there and schmooze or sell.

Fortunately, there is a solution. I call it the Personal Business Development Plan. This approach begins by recognizing personality styles. You're familiar with that concept: The Meyers Brigggs test, the DiSC profile or some other assessment tool is used to determine something you already know: Whether you're an Extrovert, Pragmatic, Analytical or Amiable. (These are my labels, every test uses its own.)

Then each person conducts a personal SWOT analysis. While SWOT (Strengths, Weaknesses, Opportunities and Threats) is typically used in business planning, there's no reason it can't be applied to an individual to determine what his or her best contribution might be.

Not all business development activities (let's expand that notion to include any activity that contributes to the 'get work' effort) involve meeting and schmoozing with strangers. A well-rounded marketing program includes research, public relations, brand-building, proposal writing, negotiation and customer service tasks, just to name a few.

Armed with the preference and aptitude information of the firm's staff and the broad spectrum of marketing and business development activities, the process becomes one of matching the right person to the right task. For example, the Extroverts might be assigned to schmoozing at the meet-and-greet receptions. The Pragmatics could look after negotiating tasks, the Analyticals can conduct market research and draft a white paper for publication and the Amiables would be naturals at customer services.

In practice it's a little more fine-grained than that. Here are some examples:

Mr. Gregarious Mixer is assigned to become actively involved in two client-based industry associations. He'll volunteer for key committees and attend at least eight monthly meetings annually. He'll have a target of meeting and launching a relationship with at least two new people each month.

Ms. Slightly Bashful agrees to attend three out of every four regular City Council meetings. She'll listen to the proceedings, become familiar with the Councilors and look for opportunities to volunteer on ad hoc committees.

Mr. Painfully Shy is going to research and write two white papers that the firm will self-publish and use as direct mailers. He'll also host a blog on the firm's website and contribute to it at least weekly.

Because each person is assigned a task for which they're suited and might even enjoy, and since everyone is only given a small, well-defined responsibility, no one ends up with a task so daunting that it cuts drastically into his or her billable time or never gets done. But by the end of the year, when everyone has done their small part, the cumulative effort and impact on your market will be huge!

Business development is like love

Remember back in high school? Remember when you were desperately in love with someone and that someone didn't even know you were on the face of the planet? What did you do?

Your high school quandary is a lot like the one you're facing now. There are people out there with whom you'd love to work, but they don't even know you exist. There are also prospects out there who know you're around but haven't recognized how talented and easy to work with you are.

Back in the high school love game, there were two schools of thought. The first group believed that love was a numbers game. If you simply asked enough girls (please excuse this seemingly sexist viewpoint, but after all, I did go through high school as a guy!) to go out with you, sooner or later someone would agree. There were two major flaws with this technique. First, it had a very high failure rate. Second, the result was often a good-news/bad news situation. The good news is, you've got a date. The bad news is, it's not someone you want to spend an entire evening with!

The second school of thought took a longer-term approach to love. You spent time thinking about the kind of girl you'd like and studying those available. When you'd found a girl who seemed nice and compatible, you set out to build a relationship.

The first step was to get her to see that you exist: Walk by her locker every day; recruit friends to make introductions; if she enjoyed music, you joined the band; if it was sports, you tried out for the team. The next was to get that first conversation. You got yourself invited to the same parties and arranged to be her lab partner in Science class. In step three you worked into expanded conversations as you sat with her at lunch in the cafeteria. Then you arranged to 'accidentally' cross paths on the street and invite her for a coffee or soda.

By this time, she's become comfortable with you, you've found some things in common and, when you ask if she'd like to go to a movie on Saturday, the likelihood of her saying, "Yes" was much higher.

Business development works the same way. Taking pot shots by submitting proposals to clients who don't already know you is a guaranteed way of being turned down. But take the time to build a trust-based relationship and you'll soon be going steady.

One More Thing...

While we're on the subject of long-ago school days, it's remarkable how much life (and business development) is like high school. In college, life was all about being an expert. "Pay attention, become an expert in this narrow field, and you'll be successful."

But it turns out that life is like high school. There, success was measured by how well you got along with people. If you were as comfortable with the kids on the track team as you were with those in the drama club, you were pretty cool. But if your only friends were the few other kids who shared your narrow interests, life at school was pretty challenging.

It was the depth and breadth of your network and friendships and the number of people who wanted you in their group that signaled success. Same rules still apply.

COMING UP IN MY NEXT BOOK

Rules are meant to be broken (or at least bent)

Most RFPs are careful to forbid you from speaking with the members of the selection committee and then go on to lay out a few other rules of the game as well.

There are some real advantages to breaking the rules, the biggest of which is that it might help you win. Let's be clear — I'm in favor of getting all the unfair advantage that's available!

Your first step to bad boy status (and just maybe winning the project) is to read the RFP carefully. Very often there will be language that lays out the rules, but then there'll be a statement to the effect that, 'notwithstanding all these rules, we get to choose who we want anyway.' In my books, when that statement is included, all's fair in love and RFPs.

Let's take that rule about not speaking with the selection committee. At the very least, call or write simply to introduce yourself, let them know that you will be submitting a proposal and are looking forward to dealing with them.

You never know, you just might gain some insight into their thoughts or feelings about the project. If someone does agree to speak with you, don't spend your time selling your firm to him or her. Instead, probe for their thoughts about the project. Listen carefully to what they want to talk about. Begin by asking some probing questions, then spend most of your time listening to the answers. You're likely to make a good impression with your listening skills.

But it's not just committee members who can be useful. Once upon a time I was helping a firm chase a transit hub project. The rules clearly stated that we were not to contact anyone on the selection committee. But one day I was doing some reconnaissance around the area where the project was to be built and came across the city's temporary transit center — a big parking lot with a collection of single-wide trailers where the buses connected and turned around. In the middle of the parking lot, directing traffic and looking very stressed, was the Transit Supervisor. At her next break I offered to buy her coffee. Over

114

the next 15 minutes I gained more insight into the issues surrounding that project than could ever have been gleaned from the RFP or the 'official' sources. All for the price of a much appreciated cup of coffee.

A few days later I got a call from the guy coordinating the RFP, who rapped my knuckles for bending the rules. I apologized profusely (nudge, nudge, wink, wink) and we went on to win the job.

Always check the rules. Then think about the advantages and consequences of bending or breaking them. Yes, it can be risky. But if you can win some truly valuable insight, or make a positive impression during your conversations, that risk may well be worth it.

Welcome to blüStone Marketing, Inc.

blüStone Marketing, Inc. (formerly Stone and Company) provides consulting, training and coaching in marketing, business development and sales for professionals in the architecture and engineering professions.

We work with private design firms and the many associations representing them. Our largest client has annual revenues in excess of $2 billion. Our smallest has been a one-person operation. We have worked in 49 our of 50 states (please help us make it all 50!), 7 our of 10 Canadian provinces and half the populated continents.

ABOUT THE AUTHOR

David Stone is a seasoned veteran of the design and construction industry.

He began his career in the mid-70s, earning degrees in Environmental Studies and in Architecture, then working for 15 years as a manager, a principal, and an owner. In 1992 he developed a specialty in marketing, sales and business development for AE firms. He has been the VP of Marketing and Sales for both a $250 million construction company and an international design firm, a Senior Consultant, speaker and trainer with PSMJ Resources and with FMI Corporation, and has been the founder and leader of his own consulting firm.

One of the foremost marketing thinkers in the AEC industry, he has advised and worked closely with hundreds of design and construction firms around the globe, ranging in size from one person to thousands, and in annual revenues from next to nothing to $2 billion. He is the author of 14 books on marketing, project management, and negotiation, and is a regular speaker at national and international design and construction industry conferences

Made in the USA
San Bernardino, CA
06 September 2018